The History of the United States, 2nd Edition

Part II

Professor Allen C. Guelzo

THE TEACHING COMPANY ®

PUBLISHED BY:

THE TEACHING COMPANY
4840 Westfields Boulevard, Suite 500
Chantilly, Virginia 20151-2299
1-800-TEACH-12
Fax—703-378-3819
www.teach12.com

ISBN 1-56585-764-X

Allen C. Guelzo, Ph.D.

Professor of American History, Eastern University

Dr. Allen C. Guelzo is the Dean of the Templeton Honors College at Eastern University, on Philadelphia's Main Line, where he is also the Grace Ferguson Kea Professor of American History. He holds an M.A. and a Ph.D. in history from the University of Pennsylvania, an M.Div. from Philadelphia Theological Seminary, and an honorary doctorate in history from Lincoln College in Illinois. Dr. Guelzo's special field of interest is American intellectual and cultural history in the period between 1750 and 1865. He has published several books on subjects in this period, including *Edwards on the Will: A Century of American Philosophical Debate* (1989); *For the Union of Evangelical Christendom: The Irony of the Reformed Episcopalians* (1994), which won the 1994 Outler Prize; *The Crisis of the American Republic: A New History of the Civil War and Reconstruction* (1995); and *Abraham Lincoln: Redeemer President* (1999), which won the Lincoln Prize. His essays and reviews have appeared in *American Historical Review, Journal of American History, William and Mary Quarterly, The Wilson Quarterly, Journal of the Abraham Lincoln Association, Civil War History, Journal of the Early Republic, Filson Club History Quarterly, Journal of the History of Ideas, Pennsylvania Magazine of History and Biography*, and *Anglican and Episcopal History*.

Dr. Guelzo has held fellowships from the American Council of Learned Societies, the Pew Evangelical Scholarship Initiative, the Charles Warren Center for American Studies at Harvard, and the James Madison Fellows Program at Princeton. He is a senior research associate of the McNeil Center for Early American Studies at the University of Pennsylvania. He serves as a member of the Board of Directors of the Abraham Lincoln Association, the Abraham Lincoln Institute of the Mid-Atlantic, the Lincoln Studies Center at Knox College (Illinois), and the Historical Society of the Episcopal Church and as a member of advisory panels for the President Lincoln and Soldiers Home Project, National Trust for Historic Preservation, the Abraham Lincoln Presidential Papers, Library of Congress, and the Abraham Lincoln Bicentennial Commission. Dr. Guelzo has also contributed articles for *The Historical Times Illustrated Encyclopedia of the Civil War, Encyclopedia of African American Religions, Routledge*

Encyclopedia of Philosophy, The Biographical Dictionary of the Union, The Encyclopedia of the Enlightenment, The Encyclopedia of American Intellectual and Cultural History, and *The American National Biography,* as well as journalism for *Civil War Times Illustrated, The Philadelphia Inquirer, The Wall Street Journal, Los Angeles Times, First Things,* and *The Washington Post.*

Table of Contents
The History of the United States, 2nd Edition
Part II

The History of the United States, 2nd Edition

Scope:

This course chronicles the history of the United States from colonial origins to the beginning of the 21st century. The lectures focus on several key themes: (1) the exceptionalism of the American experiment, symbolized by the Puritan "city on the hill"; (2) the commitment to socioeconomic mobility and opportunity in the marketplace; (3) the expanding enfranchisement of citizens in the development of political democracy; and (4) the confirmation of the "melting pot" as a symbol of inclusion in the national body politic. The spread of literacy and mass information, the political and cultural importance of regionalism, and the central role of civilian government are also salient themes in the lectures that follow.

This portion of the Teaching Company's *History of the United States* survey course carries you from the beginnings of European settlement of what is now the United States to the end of the Mexican War and the Great Compromise of 1850. It covers, in other words, what historians like to call "Colonial America" and the "Early Republic." The 36 lectures in this first part are built around four important themes:

1. How did the experience of discovery and settlement change Europeans, American native peoples, African and Caribbean slaves, and all the other different and sometimes hostile populations that came (or were forced to come) to North America into an entirely different kind of people, the Americans? In what ways has that made America exceptional and unique among the other, older nations of the West and of the world?

2. How did the United States manage to assimilate so many different peoples from so many different places?

3. How did the geography, beliefs, and necessities of the settlements Europeans planted along the eastern coast of North America develop such unprecedented religious, political, and economic freedom?

4. How did the natural resources of North America, and the human resourcefulness of its people, generate such an abundance of wealth—and so many confrontations over the way to use it?

We will begin our expedition into the American past in Lectures One and Two with the first phases of European exploration and examine why it was that a continent Europeans at first thought was a disappointment quickly became an asset. From there, in Lectures Three through Five, we will look at how Europeans turned from organizing settlements whose chief purpose was simply extraction of resources for European use to the creation of settlements of occupation, or *colonies*. English colonization, in particular, had three very different patterns for settlement in New England, the Chesapeake, and the "middle colonies." The most significant development, however, will be the way in which these colonies matured, from being stages for Europeans to make fortunes to being homes for people who were no longer really Europeans (even when they tried to be). In passing, we will see in Lectures Seven and Eight how the colonials practiced and changed religious beliefs, created various levels of culture unique to their own worlds, and struggled to decide (in Lectures Nine and Ten) whether they were simply plantations on the periphery of someone else's empire or societies that had achieved identities of their own that their European sponsors needed to respect.

Much of the first 12 lectures will be about personalities—John Smith at Jamestown, John Winthrop and Cotton Mather in Boston, William Penn and Benjamin Franklin in Philadelphia, Jonathan Edwards in his pulpit, William Billings in his singing school, John Singleton Copley at his easel, and George Whitefield on his travels. This portion of the course will also be about war—at first, brushfire wars for the survival of individual settlements, then world wars in which the colonies were expected to serve as proxies for their empires. Of course, Lectures Eleven through Thirteen will be about the war that eventually separated 13 of these colonies from Great Britain and made them a new nation, the United States.

The American Revolution appeared to be a break with the past—it cut Americans loose politically from Britain, but even more fundamentally, it cut them off from the entire European political tradition. As we will see in Lecture Fourteen, the new American nation was a child of the Enlightenment, and it was the first modern Western nation on any large scale to consciously abandon the age-old traditions of status and monarchy and experiment with an ideal form of enlightened government, a republic. But republics were a new and untested idea, and the newness of the idea was underscored by how quickly Americans developed radically different views about what a republic should look like. These views coalesce in Lectures Fifteen through Eighteen around two figures who are vitally important to these lectures: Thomas Jefferson and Alexander Hamilton. But they include a host of characters both great (George Washington) and small (William Maclay) as, of course, they should when our story is about the first great venture in popular government.

The Jefferson-Hamilton division begins a script that will be played out over Lectures Nineteen and Twenty, as Americans struggle to reconcile the impact of the Industrial Revolution with their allegiance to a republican system. Once again, it is the characters who come to the fore—Andrew Jackson, the bank-killer and apostle of agrarian democracy in Lectures Twenty-Seven through Twenty-Eight, and Henry Clay, the sophisticated statesman who, in Lecture Thirty, convinces us that the American experiment would never succeed until it built itself up as an industrial competitor of Europe. But Americans will work to find other ways of sorting out their new identity as distinct from the Old World, in literature and philosophy as much as politics. They will mark out a path of their own by giving religion an entirely new place in public life (Lecture Twenty-Five), by developing a collegiate moral philosophy that provides instruction for public virtue (Lectures Thirty-One and Thirty-Two), and by entertaining new assumptions about men and women, white and black, slave and free. And there will still be war, literal—the War of 1812 in Lecture Twenty-One; Indian war and the wars of expansion in Lectures Nineteen, Twenty-Two, and Thirty-Four; the Mexican War in Lecture Thirty-Five—and figurative—the Bank War in Lecture Twenty-Nine; the political warfare of Democrat and Whig in Lectures Twenty-Three and Twenty-Four and, again, in Lecture Thirty; the determination of abolitionists to rid America of slavery and of slaveowners to keep it in Lectures Thirty-Three and Thirty-Six.

This is the story of how to make a republic—make it in the midst of a hurricane of economic change in the late 18th and early 19th centuries, make it despite conflict and prejudice, make it so that it re-makes its own citizens into a people utterly different from anything the world has seen before—*and* how to keep it. Or, as we come to the close of Lecture Thirty-Six, how to very nearly lose it.

Lecture Thirteen
The American Revolution—Washington's War

Scope:

The Saratoga victory and the diplomacy of Benjamin Franklin in Paris persuaded France to commit itself to an alliance with the United States. This provided money, credit, weapons, and eventually, French naval and military resources to the Americans and forced the British to shift the focus of their war, evacuating Philadelphia, garrisoning New York City, and shifting active campaigning to the southern states and the West Indies. Despite early victories in the South, the British field forces under Lord Cornwallis were eventually cornered by a combined land-and-sea campaign conducted by Washington and the French at Yorktown, where the British surrendered. The Treaty of Paris in 1783 reluctantly conceded American independence.

Outline

I. The French intervention in the Revolution forced the British to completely rethink their strategic priorities.

    A. Howe's successor, Clinton, was ordered to abandon Philadelphia, withdraw to New York, and confine himself to naval operations.

        1. The Continental Army, coming out of Valley Forge, successfully harassed the retreating British at Monmouth (1778).

        2. British energies were redirected against the French in the West Indies, the New England coastline, and the western frontier.

    B. In 1778, Clinton resolved to extend his coastal operations to the South.

        1. The British occupied Savannah and the Georgia hinterland.

        2. Clinton then organized an expedition that seized Charleston.

    C. The ease of these conquests convinced Clinton that British control could be extended inland.

1. Lord Cornwallis attempted to invade North Carolina but was stopped at King's Mountain (1780).
2. Cornwallis's second attempt met with defeats at Cowpens and Guildford Courthouse (1781).
3. Cornwallis attempted to set up a new base for operations at Yorktown, only to be hemmed in by French and American troops and forced to surrender, effectively eliminating the only sizable British land force left in America (1781).

II. The impact of the war was felt even before it had ended.
   A. The American economy was seriously disrupted.
      1. American shipping was hard hit and lost its former protection on the high seas from the British Navy.
      2. Slaves deserted southern plantations to join the British.
      3. The attempt to create an American currency was wrecked by disastrous inflation.
   B. American politics on the local level were increasingly radicalized.
      1. The old colonial elite was either exiled or deposed.
      2. New state constitutions experimented with democratic politics.

III. The Treaty of Paris (1783) ended by recognizing American independence.
   A. The British conceded the legal existence of the colonies.
      1. British possessions west of the Appalachians were ceded to the United States.
      2. Franklin asked that Canada be ceded to America in return for a separate peace with Britain.
   B. Washington set an example by resigning from the army.
      1. Many of the officers had supported a military intervention to end mismanagement by Congress.
      2. Washington set an example of virtuous republicanism that probably saved the Confederation.

Essential Reading:

Conway, *The War of American Independence*, chapters 5–6.

Supplementary Reading:

W. B. Allen, ed., *George Washington: A Collection*, chapter 5.

James Thomas Flexner, *George Washington in the American Revolution.*

Questions to Consider:

1. Was it a blessing that the Continental Army had lost so many battles that it was not able to pose a political threat until the close of the war?

2. What roles did the interventions of France, the Netherlands, and Spain play in obtaining independence for the United States?

Lecture Thirteen—Transcript
The American Revolution—Washington's War

The French Alliance forced the British to completely rethink their strategic priorities in dealing with their rebellious colonies. Sir William Howe was replaced in command of the British armies in North America. He actually resigned in protest because of all the stinging criticism he had received for the surrender of Burgoyne, when he should have been meeting Burgoyne in New York, and demanded an investigation in England to justify his conduct. In any case, Howe was very soon off the scene, and Sir Henry Clinton was promoted in his place as commander of the British Army in North America. Clinton would withdraw the British Army from Philadelphia, and the bulk of it would be sent to the West Indies to carry the war to the French islands in the Caribbean. Only a reduced force would be maintained in New York City, and Clinton was to use New York City and those remaining troops as the base for mounting raids along the American coast just to keep the pressure up.

As far as a major theatre of warfare, the British had now been forced to turn their attention to dealing with the French in other places in the world. The British marched out of Philadelphia on June 28, 1778, and headed for New York City with 3,000 loyalists packing their bags and leaving Philadelphia behind them. George Washington struck his winter camp in Valley Forge and, looking for an opportunity to cut off part of the slow-moving British column, he looked for an opportunity; he pounced on it on June 18, near Monmouth, New Jersey, when he attacked the British rear guard, under the command of Lord Charles Cornwallis.

The officer to whom he delegated the attack botched the job, and in short order Clinton had turned around with his main column to rescue Cornwallis. Suddenly, it was the Americans who looked like they were being cut off, but then Washington arrived on the scene to take personal command of the situation. With surprising ease, the Americans organized themselves, developed their lines, fended off Clinton's assaults, and under cover of night the British turned around and continued their march to New York City.

One the New Jersey captain enjoyed the spectacle immensely. He boasted that the Continental Army had met and fought the flower of the British Army, and succeeded in humiliating the proud king's guards and haughty British grenadiers.

Indeed they had, at Monmouth, and one reason for it was the influx of French money that allowed Washington to re-equip and retrain the Continental Army during the dreary months of winter encampment at Valley Forge. The army Washington commanded through 1776 and 1777 had been chronically under-clothed, underfed, and amateurishly officered. At one point, the shortage of muskets in the Continental Army was so acute that Washington paraded the Connecticut State Militia and confiscated all the usable muskets they possessed for the Continentals. The army that dragged itself into Valley Forge in December of 1777 faced a winter in which up to one-fourth of the army was sick, and almost another fourth was without shoes or adequate clothing to face the winter. Washington, in fact, had only 7,600 men ready for duty in February of 1778, and a third of them were on detached service at outposts scattered between Trenton, New Jersey, and Wilmington, Delaware.

The French Alliance, though, once it was formalized in February of 1778, rapidly altered the appearance of Washington's army. The French shipped 23,000 muskets to the Continentals, and French money bought the services of a cadre of veteran French and European mercenary officers: the youthful Marquis de Lafayette; Baron Johann DeKalb; the Polish hero, Thaddeus Kosciusko; and the most puzzling of them all, Baron Friedrich Wilhelm von Steuben.

Although von Steuben liked to pass himself off as a Prussian general, member of the staff of Frederick the Great, the truth was that he had never risen higher in the Prussian Army than the rank of captain. What Steuben did have, however, was nearly 20 years of experience as a junior officer in training soldiers, and that made him more valuable to the Americans than any dozen or so aristocrats in lace epaulettes. Thanks to Steuben, by the spring of 1778, the Continental Army had acquired precision, discipline, and most important—self-confidence.

The Prussian's claim to nobility might have been fraudulent, but not his claim to competence. Sir Henry Clinton did not propose to try serious consequences with Washington's Continentals if he could help it. The British Empire had its hands full elsewhere with the French and so, as I said earlier, America began to take a back seat in this war. In September of 1778, the French launched a series of attacks on the British islands in the West Indies, capturing the islands of Dominica, which they had lost at the end of the French and Indian

War; St. Vincent; and Grenada. The American sea captain, John Paul Jones, took a French squadron raiding along the English coast, and in September of 1779, Jones challenged and captured a British frigate, *HMS Serepis*, in exactly the kind of stand-up fighting at sea that the Royal Navy had never expected to lose.

In April of 1779, Spain joined the alliance, hoping, in the event of a British defeat, to recover control of Gibraltar. This meant that Britain was now stretched fatally thin, and America fell from being the chief object of British attention to being somewhere in the middle.

This did not keep Sir Henry Clinton from doing his best to at least keep the Americans off balance. In December of 1778, peeling off about 3,000 men from his small garrison in New York City, Clinton sent a raiding expedition against Savannah, Georgia. The surprised Americans defending Savannah offered a brief resistance and then ran, leaving Savannah and a good portion of the Georgia hinterland open to British occupation. It had taken, in fact, so little effort to capture Savannah that the British promptly turned and lunged northward at Charleston in the summer of 1779, and even briefly laid siege to Charleston.

The following summer, Clinton himself personally took charge of the British troops in Georgia, marched northward again, and this time forced the surrender of Charleston on May 12, 1780, with 2,500 Continental soldiers falling into his hands as prisoners. Carolina loyalists now came flocking to Clinton's banner, and one group of loyalists in particular were organized as the British Legion, under the command of a colorful young British cavalry officer, Banastre Tarleton.

Tarleton's legion quickly acquired a particular reputation for evening up scores with their fellow Americans. Under Tarleton's orders, for instance, loyalists massacred a detachment of 350 Continentals at the Waxhaws at the end of May. If this kept up, Sir Henry Clinton would be able to roll up the rebel colonies one by one, this time doing it from the South rather than trying to do it from the north. Clinton organized other raids along the New England coast in the summer of 1778, one of them hitting New Bedford, another New Haven, Fairfield, and Norwalk, another New London.

Unlike Howe or Gage, Clinton felt no inclination to go easy on the Americans. Deprived of reinforcements, shoved to the back of the strategic shelf, Clinton and his officers took out their frustrations on their opponents and their property. The raids on New Bedford and New Haven included widespread burning, looting, destruction, and not only there. Handsome bribes and promises allowed British agents to recoup their Iroquois Confederation in New York, to rampage through the unprotected New York and Pennsylvania frontiers. The Cherokees were also promised, bribed, and encouraged to harass the backwoods of Georgia and the Carolinas. Tribes like the Shawnee, the Miami, and the Wyandotte were intended to attack Virginia's most extended settlements across the Appalachians in Kentucky.

Promises of freedom were also offered to slaves who would run away to the British lines, and in some cases the newly freed slaves, like the so-called Colonel Ty and his Black Brigade, took the king's shilling and served the British Army as scouts, engineers, and raiders in New York and New Jersey. Lord Dunmore, the last Royal Governor of Virginia, even briefly recruited an Ethiopian regiment of runaway slaves to turn and then fight their former masters. The success of the British in the South, the success of the British in causing havoc on the frontier and on the coastlines, as you can imagine, set beside the comparative inactivity of Washington around New York City, had the usual malcontents applauding and the usual tongues wagging.

Over Washington's disapproval, Congress split off 1,400 Continentals from Washington's command and sent them south in June of 1780, where Horatio Gates, the victor of the Battle of Saratoga, was appointed as overall American commander. Gates quickly proved how well placed Washington's disapproval had been. The main British force in the Carolinas had been turned over by Sir Henry Clinton to Lord Cornwallis while Clinton returned to directing operations in New York City, and on August 16, Cornwallis handily defeated Gates at the Battle of Camden, South Carolina. Gates, in fact, was so badly beaten that Gates himself mounted a horse and rode, without stopping, 60 miles to Charlotte, North Carolina, riding, in the process, right out of any hope of further military glory. "This country is entirely conquered," crowed one British officer, "The people crowd in from all quarters to deliver up their arms."

Well, that was, of course, an illusion. In real terms, Cornwallis had too few men to hold the American territory that he now controlled, much less to think of conquering more. He was reminded of this in

October, when a loyalist force of 1,200 men under Major Patrick Ferguson was attacked at King's Mountain in western North Carolina by American militia; the militia surrounded the loyalists, overran their position, and—remembering what Tarleton and the British Legion had done to the Waxhaws—hanged nine of the loyalist leaders as traitors. The loss of Ferguson and his loyalist legion forced Cornwallis to pull back and winter in South Carolina, where lack of supplies and raids by American guerrillas like Francis Marion—the so-called Swamp Fox—and Thomas Sumter, they together made winter quarters as miserable for the British as the British had made winter quarters miserable for the Americans at Valley Forge.

Sir Henry Clinton had his own troubles in New York City and little to spare for the aid of Cornwallis. In an effort to break Washington's grip around New York City, Clinton attempted to seize the strategic American forts above the city at Stoney Point and Paulus Hook, and he did capture them, only to have Washington just as easily recapture them. Clinton then tried again by bribing a senior American general, Benedict Arnold, to betray the Continental's outpost on the Hudson River at West Point.

Benedict Arnold had served with a good deal of bravery in the disastrous Quebec Expedition in 1775, and he probably deserved more credit for the Saratoga victory than did Horatio Gates, but Arnold, despite that distinguished record, was in debt—he had married a loyalist wife—and above all he was embittered by what he saw as Congress's unwillingness to reward his military genius with the sort of command he thought he deserved. Thus, he joined hands with Clinton to betray West Point, a plot that nearly worked until Clinton's adjutant general—Major John Andre—was captured by the Continental Army as Andre tried to slip through the American lines, in civilian clothes, with papers for Arnold. Andre was hanged, but Arnold escaped to New York City, where he completed his turn of coat by commanding a British raid on the Chesapeake at the end of 1780.

Cornwallis' misery in South Carolina might have been easier to bear if he had realized that the Continental Army was also in some unhappy straits. It was becoming something close to a habit for the Continental Congress to lose interest in the army whenever it went into winter quarters, and Washington's men had to endure two more freezing, hungry winters in 1779 and 1780. Of course, there were also sporadic mutinies over pay because pay, more often than not, was simply not forthcoming from Congress.

Seventeen-hundred Pennsylvania Continentals actually set off for Philadelphia to confront the Congress directly, and an amused Sir Henry Clinton, in New York City, actually sent two emissaries through the lines in civilian clothes (this was all done in secret) to offer these rebellious Continentals full pardons and pay if they would desert to the British, but the Pennsylvanians wanted redress of grievances, not commission of treason. They hanged Clinton's emissaries and, on the strength of promises from George Washington, they went back to camp.

The same happy result, the same happy ending, could not be applied to Lord Cornwallis. In January of 1781, Cornwallis had only 1,300 men ready for duty, and not more than 3,000 British soldiers all told under his immediate command. There was another 5,000 British soldiers in Charleston and Savannah, but they were needed to guard those positions, especially now that the French Navy was hovering off the American coasts and could sweep down the moment one of those garrisons was weakened. It was that French Navy that now impelled Cornwallis to his most difficult decision.

Unable to draw supplies overland from Charleston or from Savannah due to Francis Marion and the American guerrillas, Cornwallis planned to set up a new base at Wilmington, North Carolina, right where the Cape Fear River empties out into the Atlantic. There, Cornwallis believed that he would be in a perfect position to receive supplies and reinforcements by sea. There, he could reopen communications with Sir Henry Clinton in New York, and there he could set about new plans for redeeming the Carolinas for Great Britain.

All of that might have worked if Cornwallis was still facing someone like Horatio Gates, but Cornwallis was not facing Horatio Gates anymore. Gates was officially relieved of command at the end of 1780 and replaced by one of Washington's favorite officers, Nathaniel Greene, a Rhode Islander who, in fact, was the youngest general in Washington's army. Greene, like so many of the rest of Washington's officers, had had no training whatsoever in military affairs before the Revolution. His family members, in fact, were Quakers, and therefore pacifists, but Greene was a quick and a nimble learner. He had what turned out to be a natural aptitude for military command.

Greene dangled one part of his army of Continentals and militia north of Cornwallis's march route, the route Cornwallis would normally have taken toward Wilmington. Greene dangled them to the north of Cornwallis's route, to decoy Cornwallis away from the coastline. Cornwallis took the bait, and detached Tarleton and 1,100 men to crush what Cornwallis assumed was an isolated and unsuspecting body of American militia.

Instead, what Tarleton found at Hannah's Cowpens on January 17 were 700 Continentals and militia under the famous and wily rifleman—Daniel Morgan. Morgan lured the reckless and overconfident Tarleton onward with what seemed to be a helpless, confused stream of untrained militia as skirmishers; Tarleton looked at them and decided this was yet another opportunity to ride right down and over more Americans, but once Tarleton was committed to the attack, the militia then stepped aside to reveal Morgan's Continentals, who proceeded to shred Tarleton's ranks as they advanced to the bayonet charge. Then, the militia closed the trap by curling around Tarleton's flanks, and Tarleton's loyalists and regulars collapsed. Only 140 mounted troopers, including Tarleton himself, managed to escape.

Cornwallis could ill afford a disaster like that at Cowpens, but at the same time he could afford still less to sit where he was. Greene closed off Cornwallis's plan to head for the coast; this forced the British to keep swinging inland and exhaust themselves, in a lengthy in-country march through North Carolina.

Desperate to shake off Greene, Cornwallis uncoiled and struck the Continentals at Guildford Courthouse on March 15. The British scored a technical victory. They captured four American cannons, but in the process Cornwallis had sustained twice as many casualties as Nathaniel Greene; unlike the Americans, Cornwallis had little hope of replacing them.

Cornwallis finally circled down to Wilmington on the coast in April, but he found, once he got there, that he could not stay there. The French Navy prevented the landing of the supplies that he was relying upon, and Cornwallis's best hope was then to strike northward again, this time into Virginia, where he could link hands with British forces at the Chesapeake under Major General William Phillips.

Cornwallis forced his way into Virginia, joined Phillips's troops, and then turned to establish a supply base at Yorktown on the James River Peninsula, but instead of this being Cornwallis's great opportunity to be re-supplied and renew his campaign, this turned out to be Washington's great opportunity to make sure that Cornwallis would have no further campaigns. In June of 1781, the French Army, which had been promised to America, arrived in Rhode Island, then moved over to New York City to join Washington. Taking advantage of French warships to blockade the Chesapeake Bay, Washington left a small force to keep an eye on Sir Henry Clinton in New York and marched the remainder of this combined French-American army, probably about 16,000 men, overland to Virginia. There, Washington trapped Cornwallis at Yorktown and, after three weeks of siege, Cornwallis surrendered.

There were still British troops in Charleston, Savannah, and New York City, but after Cornwallis's surrender at Yorktown, there were none to spare for offensive operations anywhere in North America, nor was Lord North's government in London in any position to offer Sir Henry Clinton any more troops to replace those lost at Yorktown.

By 1782, in fact, the war was costing Britain 20 million pounds a year to wage. The loss of trade with America caused exports in Britain to fall by 18 percent. Woolen exports in particular plummeted from a figure worth approximately £900,000 in 1772 to only £58,000 in 1776. That was the toll the war was taking on the British economy. Bankruptcies in British finance increased by approximately 200 percent between 1772 and 1778. On February 27, 1782, surveying the wreckage of its plans and hopes in North America, Parliament voted to suspend the war by a slim margin of 234 to 215. A month later, reading the handwriting on the wall, Lord North resigned as Prime Minister.

An interim government under the Marquis of Rockingham lasted only until Rockingham's death in June, when he was followed by William Petty, the second Earl of Shelburne. In turn, Lord Shelburne opened communications with Benjamin Franklin in Paris, and by November, a provisional agreement recognizing American independence had been okayed, and it was followed by a formal peace treaty in Paris on September 3, 1783. If the war did a lot of damage to the British economy, and it did, it did little good to the American economy either. During this war, American shipping, which had been—at the same time as it was being regulated—also protected by the British Navy, now became the target of its former protectors, both the navy and British privateers.

Along with that, American merchants lost the privileges they had enjoyed as British subjects while trading in Europe. At home, the simple wastage of war in South Carolina alone ran up a bill estimated at £3 million. Slaves and indentured servants deserted to the British in droves. Five thousand Georgia slaves sought refuge in Savannah after it was captured by the British. Twenty thousand South Carolina slaves sought British protection in Charleston. Even Thomas Jefferson lost 30 slaves to a British raiding party in Virginia.

There was also the collapsing American currency. By 1782, Congress and the states together had issued 440 million dollars in paper money, all of which was scarcely worth more than newsprint. Between 1777 and 1780, prices in some regions in America went up between 190 percent and 500 percent. How's that for inflation? Overall, per capita income in America fell by four percent between 1774 and 1790. That's the equivalent of the Great Depression.

American politics was almost as deranged by the war as the American economy. Thousands of loyalists were imprisoned by the Continental Congress or forced to flee after retreating British armies, and the disappearance of the loyalists wiped out a significant segment of the old colonial elite. In their places, the new state constitutions—adopted by state after state—undertook dramatic experiments in popular government. Philadelphia's Benjamin Rush, a signer of the Declaration of Independence, complained that the new Pennsylvania Constitution of 1776, which handed out the vote to nearly all adult males regardless of property holding, "was called a democracy when a mobocracy, in my opinion, would be more proper. All our laws breathe the spirit of town meetings and porter shops." This was coming from a friend of the Revolution, no less.

One French officer was shocked to find that, among his allies, a locksmith, a cobbler, or a merchant may become a member of Congress, and that far from this embarrassing the Americans, they were proud of it. Another French officer could scarcely contain his laughter when he hard Continental officers naively asked French generals, aristocrats all, what their trade was at home.

Well, restraining this spirit of leveling was risky, and never more risky than when Congress tried to do the restraining. The Articles of Confederation, which were gutted by Congress of all but the gentlest of controls on the states, took two years to move through Congress, and then an additional three years to be ratified by the states; the Articles of Confederation did not actually come into effect as the first American Constitution until March of 1781, only seven months before Washington accepted Cornwallis's surrender at Yorktown.

You see, it was almost easier to defeat the British Empire than to get Americans to agree on politics, but defeat the British they did, and the Treaty of Paris legally recognized the independent existence of the United States of America and ceded to it not only Britain's claims on the 13 colonies, but to all the western lands between the Appalachians and the Mississippi River—the lands won in fact from the French only 20 years before. Now, mind you, Benjamin Franklin, as part of the negotiating team for the treaty, had tried to suggest to Lord Shelburne that the British add Canada to the session as a goodwill gesture, but that went nowhere. Certainly, though, the most unlikely result of the war, and I mean this from a European view, concerned George Washington. The ineptitude of Congress and the political chaos in the states set a number of Washington's officers to whispering that the Continental Army should take matters in hand and make Washington the first king of America. They would bring order to things, and so would Washington as king.

Washington would not even listen for a moment. The army was demobilized peacefully, and Washington resigned his commission in December of 1783, desiring only to return to Mount Vernon and the life of a gentleman planter. All this was done without the slightest effort to grab the power the army would gladly have put within his reach. Instead, Washington simply rode away back into private life, not only setting an example of virtuous Whig republicanism, but probably saving the neck of the Confederation in the process. "If this is true," cried a thunderstruck King George III, "then he is the greatest man of the age." The question now became whether Washington's fellow Americans were going to be able to live up to his example.

Lecture Fourteen
Creating the Constitution

Scope:

The Revolution was not even over before the ramshackle nature of the Articles of Confederation began to show at the seams. The Continental Congress was succeeded by a Confederation Congress in which each state in the Union had an equal vote, the Confederation government had no power of taxation, and revolutionary debts to both foreign and domestic creditors went unpaid. A revolt by disgruntled farmers in western Massachusetts under Daniel Shays stimulated alarm that the Confederation might easily dissolve. A convention called in 1786 to discuss river navigation issued a recommendation to the Confederation Congress for a national convention to draw up a new constitution. The convention assembled in Philadelphia in 1787 and was dominated by nationalists, including Alexander Hamilton and James Madison, who were convinced that the American states could survive only by creating a more effective central government. The Constitution they drew up proposed a single executive president, a bicameral Congress (with one house representing the states and the other representing the population directly), and a judiciary. Anti-Federalists suspicious of central power fought the new Constitution tenaciously, but the persuasive genius of *The Federalist Papers* and the sorry experience of the Articles of Confederation overrode popular doubts. The Constitution was ratified by the states, and George Washington was inaugurated as the first president in New York City in March 1789.

Outline

I. The Revolution gave independence to 13 new states, but it was not clear whether it also created a new nation.

   A. Both Congress and the states were hopelessly in debt by the end of the Revolution.

   1. Congress had taken to paying its bills in paper money, which was hemorrhaging value.

   2. Those who lent Congress money in return for Continental securities watched the value of these pledges dwindle away to nothing.

   3. The states tried to prevent their people from using it.

4. In the summer of 1786, a rebellion led by Daniel Shays protested Massachusetts taxes.

5. Virginia's western-most settlements in Kentucky and Tennessee tried to organize their own state of Franklin.

B. But by 1785, many members of the revolutionary leadership were being replaced by a new generation.

1. They saw the nation, not the states, as the source of political authority.

2. The best example among these new men was Alexander Hamilton.

3. Under the new leadership, state constitutions began to revise the organization of power.

C. Two events finally triggered action.

1. Virginia and Maryland called a convention to discuss river navigation rights and concluded by asking for a national convention to write a new constitution.

2. The rebellion led by Shays (1787) threatened popular revolution, which the states feared they could not suppress themselves.

II. The Constitutional Convention met in Philadelphia in 1787.

A. The most obvious issue was that of power.

1. The national government was given the right to levy taxes on the states and on exterior commerce and to issue money.

2. The national government was given the power to maintain a national army and navy.

B. The second issue was who should control this government.

1. The Virginia Plan called for a two-house legislature, an executive, and a judiciary.

2. The New Jersey Plan called for a one-house legislature with each state having an equal vote.

3. The Great Compromise created two houses in the Congress, one elected according to population and the other composed of equal representation from each state.

C. The convention designed a surprisingly powerful presidency.

1. The president was responsible for executing the laws, commanding the armed forces, and supervising foreign relations.

    2. This might have been a stumbling block, had not the election process been amended so that the states elected the president through the electoral college and had it not been assumed that Washington would be the first president.

  D. The new Constitution also had some striking omissions.

    1. No allowance was made for political parties.

    2. The principle of the supremacy of the national government over the states was implied but not stated.

    3. No precise standard of citizenship was established.

III. The old radicals greeted the Constitution with a hail of abuse, but the "new men" were better organized in reply.

  A. The pro-Constitutionalists took the name *Federalist*, as though they were still sympathetic to the states.

    1. This left the old revolutionaries with no other choice but to bill themselves merely as the *Anti-Federalists*.

    2. Hamilton, Jay, and Madison undertook a propaganda campaign for the Constitution in *The Federalist Papers*.

  B. These initiatives paid off handsomely.

    1. By July 1788, the necessary number of states had ratified.

    2. Resistance was pacified by the promise of ten amendments to the Constitution, which would act as a Bill of Rights.

Essential Reading:

Hamilton, Jay, and Madison, *The Federalist*, numbers 9–10, 15, 41–43, and 57, in George W. Carey and James McClellan, *The Federalist*.

Supplementary Reading:

Lance Banning, *The Sacred Fire of Liberty*, chapter 9.

Gordon S. Wood, *The Creation of the American Republic, 1776–1789*, chapters 12–13.

Questions to Consider:

1. Why did the Anti-Federalists object so strongly to the Preamble to the Constitution?

2. What has it taken to remedy the Constitution's omissions?

Lecture Fourteen—Transcript
Creating the Constitution

The American Revolution was ended by the Treaty of Paris, but it was not so clear that the Treaty of Paris ensured the survival of the nation the Revolution had created. For one thing, both Congress and the states were hopelessly in debt by the end of the Revolution. Now, the states could hope eventually to pay their bills by taxing their citizens, but Congress? Congress had no such power under the Articles of Confederation. In addition, as I mentioned last time, it had taken to paying its bills in paper money, which, quite literally, was hemorrhaging value month by month.

The optimistic or patriotic souls who had lent Congress money had received—in return for the lending—Continental securities, Continental IOUs, or Continental currency, and they watched the value of these securities and pledges dwindle away to nothing. The veterans of the Continental Army, even after they were demobilized, still went unpaid, or else they had to accept payment in bizarre forms of promissory notes, such as quartermaster certificates.

The more the value of Continental money and Continental securities depreciated, the more the states tried to prevent their people from using it, even if that meant that individual states in effect were trying to bankrupt the Confederation government to protect themselves. Virginia and North Carolina actually taxed Continental securities in order to encourage their people to liquidate them. Maryland and New Jersey moved to take responsibility for funding their states' portion of the national debt in their own currencies. Others would refuse to accept Continental notes and securities for the payment of state taxes. In some cases, the states would offer to redeem Continental securities in state currencies so that the states would end up holding the financial paper of the Confederation government, and therefore holding the Confederation financially hostage.

Now, that didn't mean that the states were managing their economies any better. In the summer of 1786, mobs in western Massachusetts gathered to protest their state's taxes. They met attempts by state officers to sell the land of those who failed to pay at sheriff's sales with armed resistance. Led by Daniel Shays, a small army of revolutionary veterans, debtors, and small farmers marched on Springfield, Massachusetts. They tried to seize the federal arsenal at Springfield. In the end, though, Shays's men were routed by the state militia. The state government was sufficiently shaken by Shays's rebellion, however, to appeal for support to the Confederation Congress.

Congress, as Massachusetts should have expected, declined to intervene because it was powerless to do anything in the state's affairs. West of the Appalachians, Virginia's westernmost settlements in what is now Kentucky and Tennessee, tried to organize their own state of Franklin, and then debated whether they should join themselves to the Confederation or to the Spanish Empire. "Have we fought for this?" asked George Washington in near despair.

Well, Washington was not the only one with this question on his mind. A large proportion of the old revolutionaries of the 1760s and the 1770s thought of themselves as Marylanders or Pennsylvanians first, and those old revolutionaries were perfectly happy to see the Confederation kept weak and toothless. In Pennsylvania, the various committees that mobilized resistance to the British were filled with people that no upstanding colonial assembly of the old days would have tolerated in their midst. It was filled with mechanics and artisans and militiamen. At the end of the Revolution, these were the people who stepped in the leadership vacuum created by the disappearance of the loyalists. Laborers in New York and Boston organized political associations to, as they said, keep lawyers and men of learning and moneyed men from being allowed to swallow up us little folks.

The number of men in the legislatures of New Hampshire, New York, and New Jersey who were only middle class increased from one-sixth to three-fifths after the Revolution. Even the notion of liberty itself was being redefined. To the old revolutionaries, the idea of liberty meant simply that communities should have the right to govern themselves. The people whom the Revolution cast up into places of power in America defined liberty more broadly. For them, liberty meant access for everyone to the political process, and maybe even a restraint on individual wealth and property in order to ensure more general economic equality. Time and politics were ticking in yet another direction, though.

By 1785, many of the revolutionary leadership were dead, or had followed the logic of their own positions and turned their political energies back to politics in their own states. Springing up beside and around the generation of the old revolutionaries was the leading edge of a new generation who remembered little or nothing of the Stamp Act or the French and Indian War. This was a generation born in the mid-1750s or the early 1760s. For them, the great formative experience of their lives, the great experience of their youth, was not Committees of Correspondence or the Boston Tea Party, but the Revolutionary War itself and service in the Continental Army. For this new generation—these men who had done the actual fighting in the Revolution—the nation was what they had fought for, and they carried out of the Revolution an entirely different perspective on what the United States should be.

In the snows of Valley Forge, in the heat of the Carolinas, in victory, and in defeat, these teenagers and young adults from New York, Pennsylvania, Virginia, and New Jersey had shared so many common hardships that their varied local identities faded away to nothingness. They had fought and bled under one national flag, whose 13 stars and stripes proclaimed union, not division, and they had marched under the orders of one man, Congress's general— George Washington—whom they had come to adore. This new generation had learned to think continentally.

John Marshall, who was later the Chief Justice of the United States Supreme Court, and we'll meet him in a few lectures, started the Revolution as a teenaged Virginia militiaman. He enlisted in the Continental Army in 1775, and survived the winter at Valley Forge. He remembered later, "I was confirmed in the habit of considering America," America, mind you, not Virginia, "I was confirmed in the habit of considering America as my country and Congress as my government." Among these new men, no one carried these characteristics so unmistakably as Alexander Hamilton.

Hamilton was born in the British West Indies, in the island of Nevis, in 1757. There is, in fact, a good deal of uncertainty about the exact birth date, even the exact birth year. Sometimes Hamilton's birth year has been dated to 1755. The fact is that we don't actually know precisely the year in which Hamilton was born. One reason for that is that he was the illegitimate son of a feckless Scottish merchant who abandoned the family that he had in the West Indies when Alexander Hamilton was just a boy. A friendly clergyman got Hamilton a place at King's College in New York City just before the Revolution, but young Hamilton felt keenly the social stigma attached to bastards in colonial society. It's little wonder that when the Revolution began, he immediately threw in his lot with the revolutionaries. I mean, here was a man without a father making common cause with those who wanted to be without a king. He formed his own company of volunteers, was tagged by Washington to join Washington's staff as an aide, and finished his soldiering by leading a dramatic bayonet charge at Yorktown that, for all practical purposes, sealed the fate of the British defenders.

However, Hamilton was appalled at the aftermath of the Revolution. He looked on the jealousies and the competition of the individual states as a betrayal of the nation he had fought for, and he saw the state legislatures as little better than tiny red-necked oligarchies bent on stymieing progress, bent on freezing economic growth. To Alexander Hamilton, the bastard with no social rank, the only way to make his way in the world was by progress and by economic growth. Anyone who sat and talked about how it was necessary to restrain growth in the interest of equality became Hamilton's enemy.

Sooner or later, the state governments—which had hobbled Congress, and which were destabilizing the Confederation—were bound to hurt people badly enough to make them wish for a change. By the middle of the 1780s, that moment had arrived. Most of the state constitutions, which had been written in the heat of the Revolution, had created state governments that usually had a single legislative house, very broadly and popularly elected. Those governments usually had a weakened role for a governor or an executive, and also a weakened role for a system of judges. Usually, the judges were popularly elected judges rather than appointed judges, who could be recalled at will.

Now, this satisfied the demand of the revolutionaries for governments where popular majorities could hold sway without obstacle, and certainly that is consistent with the demand of the revolutionaries that taxation and other policies be based upon the activities of the people's representatives—not by a Parliament 3,000 miles away. Popular majorities are not always wise majorities, however, and timid governors and judges who keep their eyes firmly fixed on reelection are as likely to be run ragged by mobs as the old governors and judges were liable to bribery and patronage.

In 1780, Massachusetts adopted a new state constitution that split its legislature into two houses, one elected generally by the people, and the other elected on the basis of districts drawn on the basis of property taxes. These two houses were paired off to review each other's legislation. It was a case of forcing the people and the money to agree on a common course.

New Hampshire adopted a new constitution in 1784, which took the appointment process for judges, and in fact for the entire rest of the state, out of the hands of the legislature and gave it to the governor. Thomas Jefferson proposed a new Virginia constitution that gave a veto power in the legislature to a senate and created an independent lifetime judiciary.

Experience was yielding new prudence. Reform of the state constitutions only highlighted the need for reform on the level of the Confederation itself. In 1785, Virginia and Maryland signed an agreement regulating the use of the Potomac River, which of course both share as a boundary. It could have been a model for a convention governing two other commercially vital shared rivers, the Susquehanna and the Delaware.

Well, the Confederation Congress had no authority to press the Virginia and Maryland example on the other states, so it fell to Virginia and Maryland, in 1786, to call a convention at Annapolis. I mean, they did it on their own hook, which would involve delegates from Pennsylvania, New York, and New Jersey, to settle disputes over rights to the Susquehanna and Delaware Rivers.

Alexander Hamilton had won election to the New York legislature that spring. Not surprisingly, he shoehorned himself onto the state delegation headed to the Annapolis Convention. There, he persuaded the Annapolis Convention that a solution to individual interstate commercial problems was impossible, unless they were considered in a larger federal context, so the Annapolis Convention was prevailed upon to call on the Confederation Congress for the assembling of a national convention of the states in Philadelphia in May of 1787, "to devise such answers as shall appear to them necessary to render the Constitution of the federal government adequate to the exigencies of the Union."

Shays's rebellion that summer added the incentive of fear to this invitation. In February of 1787, Congress hurriedly issued an invitation to all the states to assemble and send delegations. The Philadelphia Convention was, at least as it was advertised, supposed to be about interstate trade. Very quickly, the principal problem was defined not as interstate trade, but as the Articles of Confederation. As the Articles became the problem, the solution would have to be a new instrument of national government.

This was very much a convention of new men like Hamilton. Twelve states were represented. Only Rhode Island refused the invitation. The delegates as a whole numbered some 74. Only three of those delegates had attended the Stamp Act Congress back in the 1760s; only eight of them had signed the Declaration of Independence back in 1776, and only a little more than half had served in the Continental Congress.

On the other hand, 22 of them had served in the Continental Army, three of them on George Washington's staff. These men were also very different from the artisans and working men who had framed the state constitutions. Fifty-five of the delegates to the Constitutional Convention came from the top five percent of the American wealth pyramid, and while the top of the pyramid in America, especially after the Revolution, was a far cry from the lords and landowners of Britain, still, at least two-thirds of them could still be classified as wealthy by American standards.

That had made it easy, and to a large degree cynical, to suggest that concern for ensuring that the rich would stay rich was what guided the councils of the Philadelphia Convention, but what would have made just as deep an impress on observers in 1787 was that so many of these men were unknowns, or at least unknown to the old revolutionaries and unknown to state politics. These were people, new men, who were ready to think continentally.

Now, if a new national constitution, rather than just a patching-up of the Articles of Confederation, was what was in the works, then the first and the most obvious issue for the Convention to deal with would be the fundamental question of power. If the problem of the Articles of Confederation was the lack of power, all right, fine, then what powers should a national government have?

Well, experience with the Articles of Confederation had certainly shown what powers a national government should not lack. It should not lack the power to levy taxes on states, or else it would never be able to raise revenue for itself. It shouldn't lack the power to regulate commerce between the states and with foreign countries. It shouldn't lack the sole power to issue money, or else everyone else would do it for them. And it shouldn't lack, as a means of enforcing the previous three, the power to maintain its own army and navy. This meant that there were at least four things that emerged right away from the experience of the Articles of Confederation that, it was clear, any new instrument of government had to contain.

Once those powers were granted, once the appropriate power of a national government was agreed upon, a second issue emerged: "All right, now that we've identified what powers the government should have; who should control those powers? Who should control this national government?" Discussion of this question took a form, more or less, of a debate on how a reorganized national Congress should be constructed.

The first proposal was put on the floor of the Convention only two days into its sessions, and it called for an entire junking of the Confederation Congress. As outlined by Edmund Randolph of Virginia, the Virginia Plan called for the creation of a three-part government, very similar, in fact, to the way John Locke had described the British government; instead of a three-way split of king, lords, and commons, however, Randolph proposed a Whiggish republicanized version of that division—an executive, legislative, and judicial division.

As for the new legislature—the second of those branches of those divisions—Randolph wanted to see the national legislature be a Congress with two houses. These two houses would elect the executive and the judiciary, and would have the authority to settle all questions that arose between the states.

The gaping flaw in the Virginia Plan was that it did not so much strengthen the national government as it strengthened the voice of the largest states, including Virginia, within it. Both houses of Congress were supposed to be elected on the basis of population according to the Virginia Plan. Since there were more Virginians than anyone else in the republic, Virginia would naturally come to prevail in Congress, and Virginia would always get its way. That provoked William Patterson of New Jersey, who countered Randolph with what became known as the New Jersey Plan.

The New Jersey Plan had in view a legislature, a Congress, with only one house, to which each state sent an equal number of delegates.

This had the power to please everyone, because in that case, power in Congress would be shared equally, no matter what the size of each state, no matter what the population of each state. The difficulty was that this was, after all, the basis upon which the Confederation Congress had been elected, and very few of the delegates wanted a repetition of that.

Nevertheless, the struggle over representation—the struggle, in other words—over who would control this new government, created an impasse that lasted in the Philadelphia Convention until July of 1787, when a great compromise was hammered out. Congress, under the terms of this great compromise, would have two houses, just as Edmund Randolph had asked. Only one house—the House of Representatives—would be elected by the people at large, though. The other house, the Senate, would be filled, along the lines with what William Patterson had asked, by two senators elected from each state, but elected by the legislatures of the states; this was so that one house would seem to be representative of the voice of the people in general, and the other house would be the place where the voices of the states spoke.

If this looked like a step down from Edmund Randolph's exalted notion of a national government, the Convention more than compensated for this by creating a surprisingly powerful executive. The Continental Congress had had a president, but the president of the Continental Congress was an office that involved little more than serving as the chairman of the Congress's sessions. Several of the state constitutions had tinkered with the notion of establishing an executive committee rather than vesting power in a single individual, like a governor. Whatever form a national executive might take, everybody wanted to avoid going to the other extreme and resurrecting the idea of a monarch for America.

These concerns make the executive designed by the Convention all the more surprising, because the new Constitution would vest the entire executive power in a single person, a president, who: would have general responsibility for seeing that congressional legislation was duly executed; would be Commander-in-Chief of the Army and Navy in time of war; and would be the general supervisor of the republic's foreign relations, nothing like the old Chairman of Proceedings in the Confederation Congress. Furthermore, bypassing the jealous interests of the states, the president was to be elected by the people of the United States as a whole.

This presidency struck many of the old revolutionaries as the most objectionable feature of the new Constitution. Patrick Henry protested that the tyranny of Philadelphia may be like the tyranny of George III. That might have been the fishbone that the states choked on, were it not for two concessions that were made.

First of all, the Convention amended the process whereby the president was elected, so that Americans would not vote directly for the president and thus put the states on the shelf, but they would vote indirectly. Americans would vote in their states for state electors who were supposed to represent the various candidates for president. These electors would then assemble as a college, not a "college" as an educational institution, but a "college" in the older sense of the word, which simply means an "assembly." The electors would come together as an electoral college, and then they would cast votes for whichever candidate they represented. Whichever candidate tallied up the most votes in the electoral college was to be president. In effect, this meant that while the people voted for the president, it was the states, through the state electors, who elected him.

The other concession that made the new presidency more palatable was the unspoken assumption that George Washington, a figure of universal trust, would be the president under the new Constitution. In fact, one thing that made the Philadelphia Convention as successful as it was involved the fact that Washington was invited to—and agreed to become—the chairman of the Convention. The prospect of this same man, the hero of the Continental Army, now the successful presiding officer of the Convention, the idea that this Washington would also be—as everyone assumed—the first president under the new Constitution did a great deal to disarm objections to the notion of the presidency as outlined in the new document.

Some basics of the old government were carried forward into the new one. For instance, the United States would remain a republic, one with a confederated, or federal, government. The states would not cease to exist under the new Constitution. In fact, to the contrary, they would actually retain substantial powers, including the powers to designate what civil rights their citizens could possess, and what citizenship amounted to.

Any effort in the Convention to nudge the southern states toward reconsidering the use of black slave labor was stoutly resisted. The best that Hamilton could get out of the Convention was an allowance that Congress be permitted to review the continuation of the trans-Atlantic slave trade, but even then, not before 1807.

The new Constitution was, in the end, an outline. It was remarkably spare and specific of language, but it was an outline vast in the principles it contained. It was, without question, the most innovative political document of an age remarkable for innovative political documents. The nations of Europe, handed down from centuries since the fall of the Roman Empire, had been constituted around decades and decades and centuries and centuries of legal, social, and political tradition. The Constitutional Convention created a new government in four months, constructed not of history, not of tradition, not upon race or ethnicity, but upon logical, even-handed propositions about power and politics.

The Convention finished its work on September 17, 1787, and the new Constitution was ready to go out to the states for their ratification. The Confederation Congress had specified that it would relinquish its power to a new Congress if and when the Constitution was approved by nine of the states. That proved to be harder to get than expected, if only because the old revolutionaries could now greet the new Constitution on their old and familiar turf in the states. Old Samuel Adams was irritated at the very opening of the new Constitution: "We the people of the United States..." Didn't the Convention understand that the states, not the people in general, had created the United States? "As I enter the building, I stumble at the threshold," Adams remarked.

The new men in the Convention proved as adroit in managing the ratification of the Constitution as they had in writing it, though. To sweeten their public image, they took the name of *Federalists* as the title for their pro-Constitution group, as though they were principally concerned to keep up the identity of the United States as a federation, and pose no threat to the states. The old revolutionaries were left with no alternative but to be branded with the negative title *Anti-Federalists*; that name alone meant that the opposition was halfway lost before they'd even opened their mouths.

Hamilton, along with James Madison of Virginia and John Jay of New York, undertook the work of propaganda for the Constitution by writing a series of 85 articles for the New York newspapers, between October 1787 and August 1788. *The Federalist Papers* explained, analyzed, cajoled, pleaded, and demanded on behalf of the new Constitution. They still form, today, the most brilliant commentary on the Constitution ever written.

The chief use of *The Federalist Papers*, however, was not in swaying general opinion. *The Federalist Papers* were aimed especially at the audience of lawyers and politicians who would compose the state ratifying conventions, and they hit their target well.

These advantages that new men had outlined paid off handsomely, although slowly. Delaware and Pennsylvania ratified the Constitution almost at once. Massachusetts followed on February 6, 1788, the sixth of the states to ratify. By the summer of 1788, the required nine states had been lined up.

Unhappily, Virginia, New York, North Carolina, and Rhode Island remained in the other column, and everyone knew that unless New York and Virginia embraced the Constitution, it had no hope of ever working. However, the promise of a bill of amendments that would explicitly restrain the federal government from interfering in religion, free speech, and a free press lured Virginia to ratification. In New York, Hamilton and Jay threatened the New York legislature with a promise that New York City would secede and join the new government as a separate state of its own unless the New York legislature ratified the Constitution. The threat was enough. New York ratified on July 26, 1788. With that, a new Constitution and a new government had been born. But who knew whether they would work?

Lecture Fifteen
Hamilton's Republic

Scope:

For Alexander Hamilton as the first secretary of the treasury, the virtue and liberty of the republic depended on defying the sense of suspicion and apprehension that greeted the new Constitution, first, by keeping the jealous interests of the individual states at bay and in balance, and second, by developing the republic's systems of finance, manufacturing, and commerce. Hamilton sent to Congress a series of three reports that outlined his plan for the future of the republic: *The Report on the Public Credit, The Report on the National Bank,* and the *Report on the Subject of Manufactures.* These reports sketched out a program for the new American economy. Yet Hamilton had to deal with the combined opposition of Thomas Jefferson in the cabinet and the southern agricultural interests in Congress, both of whom believed that the American future lay in independent domestic agriculture.

Outline

I.   The new Constitution was greeted with a sense of suspicion and apprehension.

   A. The United States had already gone through two ineffective governments.

      1. The Continental Congress was hardly more than an unofficial federation.

      2. The Articles of Confederation were weak and ramshackle.

   B. Support for the Constitution had to be bought with promises to the states.

      1. It had to promise to do nothing to establish a state religion.

      2. It had to promise to do nothing to restrain freedom of speech.

      3. It would do nothing to meddle in a variety of state affairs.

II. Like most political compromises, these proved impractical from the first day.

A. The Constitution made no provision for an executive staff, which meant that Washington had to create one.

1. He authorized four departments—War, Treasury, State, and Attorney General.

2. He appointed Alexander Hamilton, Thomas Jefferson, Henry Knox, and Edmund Randolph to head the newly created departments.

B. Because the new federal government had inherited war indebtedness, Hamilton had to design measures to restore the government to solvency.

1. *The Report on the Public Credit* recommended the assumption of the debt.

2. *The Report on a National Bank* recommended a public/private venture that would help pay off the debt.

3. *The Report on the Subject of Manufactures* recommended government support for manufacturing.

C. Hamilton had to deal with the combined opposition of Jefferson and Randolph.

1. In Congress, Hamilton relied on the support of members of Congress who were invested in government debt.

2. Hamilton had the authority of Washington behind him, especially concerning the national bank.

3. Jefferson resigned from the cabinet in frustration.

III. Hamilton stepped down as treasury secretary in 1795, but the decade was clearly Hamilton's.

A. Hamilton's economic plans bore early fruit.

1. Forty new corporations were chartered.

2. State legislatures chartered new banks.

3. Europeans began investing in America.

B. Nevertheless, Jefferson remained a serious opponent of the Hamiltonian vision.

1. Washington's hand-picked successor for the presidency, John Adams, barely squeaked past Jefferson in the 1796 presidential election.

2. Hamilton's friends in Congress turned out to be worse than his enemies.

Essential Reading:

The three reports in Freeman, *Alexander Hamilton: Writings*.

Supplementary Reading:

Stanley Elkins and Eric McKitrick, *The Age of Federalism.*

Forrest McDonald, *Alexander Hamilton.*

Questions to Consider:

1. In what ways does the modern American economy resemble the plan set out in Hamilton's three great reports?

2. Does Washington's role as president compare favorably or unfavorably with his achievements as a military commander in the Revolution?

Lecture Fifteen—Transcript
Hamilton's Republic

Modern Americans take the Constitution of the United States so much for granted that it becomes difficult to appreciate the sense of suspicion and apprehension with which it was greeted, when the government it created finally began to operate in the spring of 1789. Support for the Constitution of 1787 had, almost literally, to be bought with promises that in exchange for ratifying the Constitution, the new Congress that it created would pass amendments that would placate the interests of the states.

Consequently, almost its first business, when Congress assembled in New York City in the spring of 1789, was to quickly pass 10 amendments to the Constitution, which promised the states that the federal government, first of all, would do nothing to establish a national state church. That simultaneously pleased states that had no officially designated religious establishment, and it also pleased those who did have one but who feared what might happen if Congress established a different church as the official national church of the United States.

Second of all, these amendments would also promise that the federal government would do nothing to restrain freedom of speech or freedom of the press. The federal government was also supposed to do nothing to restrain the cherished republican independence of the citizens of the states by such potential outrages as restricting the creation of armed state militias, imposing search and seizure policies, quartering federal troops on private property, or in fact doing anything else that the federal Constitution did not precisely specify as a power of the federal government.

The last of these ten amendments, which became known among the ranks of those who mistrusted the new Constitution as the Bill of Rights, summed up its own promises of republican restraint by declaring that the powers not delegated to the United States by the Constitution, nor prohibited by it to the states, are reserved to the states respectively, or to the people. There was restraint that could make all of the states happy.

In December of 1790, the new president, George Washington, and Congress uprooted themselves from New York City and set up operations in the old Pennsylvania statehouse in Philadelphia. Hardly

©2003 The Teaching Company.

had Congress convened on the first Monday in December before President Washington found it necessary to circumvent what some of those amendments had promised.

A few of the ways in which Washington and the Congress in Philadelphia inched around the promises of the amendments were simply matters of necessary procedural arrangements, without which the new government could hardly have functioned at all. The Constitution, for instance, made no provision for the creation of an official presidential staff of advisors and administrators.

The sad experience of government under the Articles of Confederation had shown that some kind of administrative staff was a necessity for the executive, though, so Congress authorized Washington to create four administrative departments: War, Treasury, State, and Attorney General; Washington was to fill those offices at his discretion, which he did by appointing Alexander Hamilton as the secretary of the treasury; Thomas Jefferson to the Department of State; and his old wartime artillery chief—Henry Knox—to the Department of War; with Edmund Randolph of Virginia to serve as Attorney General.

The Constitution also created a federal judicial system, to balance the legislative powers of Congress and the president. The problem was that having brought a federal judiciary into existence, the Constitution did nothing to spell out its structure or its responsibilities, beyond providing for a federal Supreme Court, and leaving such inferior courts as might be necessary to be created by Congress.

Then there were problems that required even more dramatic end runs around the prohibitions in the Tenth Amendment. The new federal government inherited, from the Continental Congress and from the Articles of Confederation, a burden of war indebtedness from the Revolution; it amounted to over $75 million, $42 million of which was owed by the federal government to its own citizens—Americans who had bought government bonds or government securities, or who had accepted Continental IOUs for goods or services during the Revolution.

Nothing in the Constitution spelled out how the federal government was to deal with this problem, and nothing in the experience of the Continental Congress or the Articles of Confederation gave much hope that the states would. The states, mind you, had their own war debt to pay off, and they were not going to welcome a rival in settling those debts in the form of the federal government in Philadelphia. There was no sign that the states were going to permit much leeway to the federal government in dealing with this problem of indebtedness. Alexander Hamilton, however, saw in the federal debt crisis not only an opportunity to serve the nation and prove himself as the secretary of the treasury, but also a means for pushing the shape of the new republic into the mold of his own particular sense of what a republic should be. For Hamilton, the survival of the American republic depended on keeping the jealous interests of the individual states at bay and in balance, while the independence of the United States was linked to how successfully the republic could develop its own systems of foreign commerce, manufacturers, and credit.

In January of 1790, in response to a directive from Congress for proposals on dealing with the debt crisis, Hamilton sent to Congress the first in a series of three reports, all of which outlined his plan, the secretary of the treasury, not only for dealing with the problem of federal government debt, but in effect what he did was to sketch out the financial future of the United States.

The first of these three reports, *The Report on the Public Credit*, Hamilton sent to Congress in January of 1790. In this report, Hamilton addressed the debt crisis head on. He rejected outright the coy suggestions from the states that the federal government simply repudiate all responsibility for the war debt. They suggested that the war debt had been contracted under two previous American governments—the Continental Congress and then the Confederation Congress. Therefore, they said, the war debt was not the responsibility of the new constitutional government, and could be repudiated entirely. If you happened to hold Continental IOUs, or if you happened to hold securities issued by the Confederation Congress, too bad for you, we're sorry, but that's the necessary sacrifice you get to make for America to be what it is. The states suggested, as an alternative, to offer to redeem the Continental securities, but to offer to redeem them at a few pennies on the dollar, or to allow the individual states to divide up the national debt among themselves and pay it off out of their own state tax revenues.

Not only would these suggestions hurt directly American citizens and war veterans who had bought these securities or taken these IOUs in good faith, but, Hamilton argued, to do any of those things would irreparably damage the trustworthiness of the new American government on the markets of the world hardly before it had begun operating. On the other hand, Hamilton was aware that there were many people in the states who welcomed precisely these conclusions on the grounds that, first of all, dealing in securities was a phony form of wealth. Dealing in securities was little better than gambling. It deserved no public respect. If anybody lost money because they'd bought government securities or invested in Continental IOUs, well, it served them right. They should never have been dealing in phony forms of wealth like that in the first place. Then, there were voices that in the states believed that anything that weakened the federal government—or kept it weak—necessarily strengthened the individual states.

With those objections in mind, Hamilton insisted to Congress that Congress must not only fund the existing war debt, but it must also assume—in other words, it must take over—the war debts owed by the states as well. Now, to deal with this added burden, Hamilton proposed three immediate solutions. First of all, raise federal taxes in the form of tariffs on imports. Then impose—and this horrified the agricultural interests—25 percent excise tax on whiskey. Now, you might wonder, why whiskey? Well, whiskey because whiskey was a major agricultural byproduct.

He then proposed the creation of a daring scheme of national banking, which leads us to his second report on December 13, 1790. Funding and managing the national debt was actually a procedural matter. Hamilton could have handled all that solely through the Treasury, but Hamilton doubted that merely raising taxes would bring in enough revenue to pay off the debt. Anyway, Hamilton was pursuing bigger political quarry.

If *The Report on the Public Credit* was actually a mechanism for putting the states in their proper places, then this second report, which was technically an extension of *The Report on the Public Credit*, but is usually better known simply as *The Report on the National Bank*, was an even bigger mechanism for creating not just a means of funding the war debt, but of creating a National Republican economy. Before 1776, no banks of any description had existed in

British North America. The reasons for this strange absence—although somewhat opaque to modern eyes, since we're used to a bank on every corner and it's hard for us to imagine a world in which there aren't any—seem opaque to us, but they were very clear to Anglo-Americans in the 18th century. After all, banks are fundamentally a legal means by which groups of individuals pool their private wealth and then make it available to large-scale entrepreneurs to borrow, and when they've borrowed it, create large-scale enterprises. In the end, the bank receives large-scale profits from the proceeds of those particular enterprises.

The British government, in the colonial days, was suspicious of anything that would permit big concentrations of wealth in the colonies because that might be a threat to the home islands. It might start making the colonies self-sufficient, and as we all know, terrible things might happen to Parliament as a result of that. If great concentrations of wealth in the colonies are a threat to the authority of Parliament, then you should not have banks in the colonies.

It wasn't just the British who adopted this attitude on a pragmatic basis, though. There were also American thinkers, American republicans, like Thomas Jefferson, who feared that banking infected people with a speculative fever, a desire to deposit money into banking pools in the false hope of attaining unreal wealth. Now, what made banking even more suspicious to the British and to Thomas Jefferson was the balance that banks struck between specie and paper. Now, in theory, banks make their money by having depositors lend them real money in hard gold and silver coin or specie. The bank then lends out not the depositors' specie, but bank notes, in other words, promise payment in specie upon demand by the holder. The bank's notes thus become the circulating currency of commercial enterprise.

Now, this, of course, if it had happened in the colonies, would have raised British suspicions that the colonists were attempting to create their own currencies, their own domestic economies. It did raise Jefferson's suspicions that banks were dealing only in illusory and artificial forms of wealth. I mean, what else was paper money? It's just paper. It's not real. The fact that banks would take gold and silver and then turn around and start dealing out to people paper money struck Jefferson as odd and suspicious.

The fact was, though, that without the kind of large-scale pooling of capital that banking makes possible, no kind of major economic growth could happen in America, which, ironically, satisfied both agricultural purists like Jefferson and British colonial administrators.

It did not satisfy Alexander Hamilton. Now that the United States no longer operated under the restraint of British law, Hamilton now proposed to provide for precisely the concentrations of capital that he believed were the only way toward American economic vigor and independence. *The Report on the National Bank* sketched out for Congress the creation of a joint public sector/private sector venture, a Bank of the United States, in which both the federal government and private investors would pool funds. The federal government would provide one-fifth of the capitalization from its own revenues. In return, the federal government would use the Bank of the United States as its instrument, as its agency, for receipt and disbursement of funds.

What was even more, the federal government would use the bank's paper notes as the national paper currency. The federal government's involvement in the Bank of the United States would guarantee its soundness for private investors. The remaining four-fifths of the bank's capitalization that private investors contributed would then be available for lending out to entrepreneurs and to business to fuel economic development. The profits that the bank then earned from those entrepreneurs would not only enrich the private depositors, the four-fifths of the capitalization, but would also then help pay off the remaining federal debt in proportion to the federal government's one-fifth holding of the bank.

Now, the most obvious question that the creation of the bank posed was: In whose interest is this national bank going to operate? Hamilton answered that question in the last of his three reports at the end of 1791, *The Report on the Subject of Manufactures*. Here, Hamilton plainly declared his intention to build American manufacturing up to a par with American agriculture, and he argued against the glorification of agricultural labor and agricultural landholding, which played so large a role in Jefferson's thinking. Jefferson had been born to landholding. Hamilton, of course, had not. Thus, it seemed to Hamilton that Jefferson's worship of agriculture was peculiar and out of place. Hamilton wrote in this third report, "The foregoing considerations seem sufficient to establish as general propositions that it is the interest of nations to diversify the industrious pursuits of the individuals who compose them."

In other words, let's not have the United States put all its chips on agriculture, economically speaking. The establishment of manufacturers is calculated not only to increase the general stock of useful and productive labor, but even to improve the state of agriculture in particular, certainly to advance the interests of those who are engaged in it. Hamilton's main devices for the establishment of manufacturers in the American republic were, first of all, the Bank of United States that he had proposed in the second report because the Bank of the United States would make a tremendous pool of government and private investment capital available for entrepreneurs to borrow from—and build—a system of manufacturers.

In addition, Hamilton proposed to juggle the new tariff system so that the tariff system would increase the cost to Americans of importing foreign manufactured goods and make the purchase of American-made goods more attractive at home. He also encouraged lifting barriers to immigration. Why? Because that would permit the recruitment of a cheap labor force for manufacturing. Again, remember, as I'd said earlier in this series, the great dilemma of the American landscape was that there was so much landscape and so little labor. This was still a problem that Hamilton was dealing with when he talks about manufacturing. Therefore, he set out to relieve the restrictions on immigration because that was where the labor force was going to come from.

Hamilton's proposals in these three reports were, to put it mildly, politically daring, but they were also financially risky, because there were no guarantees that any of this was going to work. Hamilton also had to deal with the combined opposition of Thomas Jefferson in the cabinet, and most of the southern agriculturists in Congress.

Jefferson saw at once that Hamilton's program was heavily biased in favor of urban financial interests, and that roused in Jefferson's mind the specter of the republic soiling its hands in merchandising and shuffling paper bank notes. The taxation scheme that Hamilton asked for was seen by Jefferson as a dagger at the security and independence of the republican farmer. The merchants who had become the primary beneficiaries of a Bank of the United States and a new American manufacturing movement would quickly turn their artificial, phony economic power in the direction of bribery and political corruption. Everything would become the same Whig nightmare it had been in the 1760s.

Jefferson announced that banks existed only to enrich swindlers at the expense of the honest and industrious. Nathaniel Macon of North Carolina sneered at banks as gaining shops where cunning projectors schemed to live off the labors of others. In any case, Jefferson argued, even if banks didn't do those terrible things, the Constitution had still given Congress no authority to create a national bank. Under the provisions of the Bill of Rights, the entire proposal for the establishment of a national bank was unconstitutional from the start.

As for encouraging domestic manufacturing, the acerbic John Randolph of Roanoke, together with Jefferson, could only snarl that agriculture—and not manufacturing—was what made the republic what it was. Randolph wrote, "The agriculturists," not the bankers, not manufacturers, "bear the whole brunt of taxation and remain poor, while the others run in the ring of pleasure and fatten upon them. The manufacturer is the citizen of no place or anyplace," and parenthetically, therefore, is not to be trusted. "The agriculturist has his property, his land, his all, while the commercial speculators live in opulence, whirling in coaches and indulging in palaces. Alert, vigilant, enterprising, and active, the manufacturing interests are collected in masses and ready to associate at a moment's warning for the many purposes of general interest to their body. Do but ring the fire bell, and you can assemble all the manufacturing interests of Philadelphia in 15 minutes. For that matter, they are always assembled, and compare notes and lay plans and possess in trick and intelligence what in the goodness of God to them the others can never possess."

Despite the opposition in both the cabinet and in Congress, Hamilton eventually negotiated the recommendations of all three reports through Congress, largely on the basis of two important assets. One of these assets was a large group of Congressmen in both the House and the Senate who had made substantial investments in government securities during and after the Revolution and who stood, quite frankly, to lose badly if Hamilton's funding and assumption proposals were not endorsed. As a result, even though the assumption proposals went down in defeat in April of 1790, the funding proposals passed through Congress in June. Then, over the summer, Hamilton swung a remarkably un-virtuous and un-republican deal with Thomas Jefferson, offering to swap Jefferson's support for assumption for Hamilton's support for a scheme to relocate the national Capitol from Philadelphia to a site on the Virginia-Maryland border. A month later, a resurrected assumption bill glided through the Senate.

Hamilton's other major asset in this process was George Washington, who had learned to trust Hamilton as a staff officer during the Revolution and who trusted him now. That trust was tested in February of 1791 when a 20-year charter for the Bank of the United States was passed by the House and sent to Washington for his signature. Within the cabinet, Jefferson and Edmund Randolph appealed to Washington to veto the bank charter, on the grounds that Congress had no authority under the Constitution to charter corporations of any sort. "Where," they asked, "in the Constitution does it explicitly state that Congress has the power to charter corporations, much less bank corporations?" Therefore, the bank's charter would violate the Bill of Rights.

Hamilton argued back to Washington that the Bill of Rights did not mean to do away with certain implied powers that are simply by common sense necessary to normal government. The Constitution, clearly, unambiguously, granted the federal government the right to regulate commerce. On the other hand, it nowhere specified that Congress should establish lighthouses and docks and buoys and fund a Coast Guard. Yet, Congress had gone ahead and enacted legislation for providing for all of these. Why? Because these facilities and these services were reasonable means toward the end of regulating commerce.

Now, just so with the bank. Yes, Congress had no express power to charter a national bank, but it did have a constitutional responsibility to regulate currency and bankruptcy; it is so specified in Section 8 of the Constitution. Hence, the authority to charter a national bank was implied in the Constitution. When the Constitution designates the end, it also implies the means to achieve that end. Washington listened and then signed the bank bill on February 25, 1791. In frustration, Jefferson waited until the end of 1793 and then resigned from Washington's cabinet.

Hamilton did not actually the cabinet for much longer. He stepped down as secretary of the treasury at the end of January 1795, but by then, his work was really done. In 1791 and in 1792, 40 new corporations were chartered in the United States—nine of them for banks and the rest for public works, canals, and turnpikes, and all of them capitalized in large measure by the bank notes and the securities issued through the Bank of the United States.

By 1815, state legislatures had copied this by chartering over 200 banks. Abroad, the value of American bonds and American securities received the highest ratings on the Amsterdam financial markets, with the result that European silver and gold specie now began to flow into the vaults of the Bank of the United States because American securities were now worth owning in Europe.

Jefferson was not placated by a success that appeared to him to be concocted out of fiscal mirages, however. In western Pennsylvania, restless farmers greeted the collectors of the whiskey excise with coats of tar and feathers, and when, in 1796, Washington announced his permanent retirement from political life, the ensuing presidential election created a riot of political confusion.

When the dust had finally settled, Washington's vice president and hand-picked successor, John Adams of Massachusetts, only barely squeaked past Thomas Jefferson, who was by now an unlooked-for freak in the Constitution's electoral provisions became Adams's vice president. The 1790s, the first decade of the new American Constitution, clearly belonged to Alexander Hamilton. Even before the decade was over, however, confusion and hostility to Hamilton's program was mounting, and as it turned out, Hamilton's friends, even more than Hamilton's enemies, would come within an ace of undoing Hamilton's republic.

Lecture Sixteen
Republicans and Federalists

Scope:

The most unforeseen development in the new republic's political life was the formation of political parties. The idea of *party* suggests that there are very different, perhaps irreconcilable, solutions to the problems of the public good, and the threat this posed to the Founders was that parties might thrive on sanctioning and perpetuating disagreements and disunion. James Madison became the organizer of the *Democratic-Republicans*, while Thomas Jefferson became their most important figurehead. Borrowing the name *Federalist* from the papers he had written in defense of the Constitution, Hamilton recruited his own Congressional supporters into a party. Yet Hamilton's skill in formulating public policy did not always translate into making party politics work. The Whiskey Rebellion and the Jay Treaty embarrassed the Federalists, who only barely managed to elect their candidate, John Adams, as Washington's successor in 1796.

Outline

I. The formation of political parties was the most important detail unforeseen in the Constitution.

   A. In the 1790s, politics was dominated by faction, not party.

      1. Faction politics is temporary; parties are built around long-term, comprehensive goals.

      2. Faction politics is local or oriented toward special interests; parties organize broad constituencies.

      3. Faction politics is small scale; parties are large scale.

      4. Faction politics is personal; parties survive the loss or defeat of leaders.

   B. The idea of *party* was an offense to the republican ideology.

      1. Party politics cuts across the grain of the republican commitment to virtue.

      2. Party politics appeals to self-interest.

      3. Republicanism assumed that politics could point only in a single, non-partisan direction, rather than sanctioning competing directions.

4. Republics are fragile because they lack hierarchy, which makes them vulnerable to party corruption.

II. No one set out to create parties, but the split between Hamilton and Jefferson was so large that it made party formation inevitable.

    A. James Madison organized the Democratic-Republicans in Congress; John Beckley was their local organizer.

        1. Opposition to Hamilton in Congress was mobilized.

        2. Local campaigns employed publicity and get-out-the-vote organizing.

        3. By 1793, there were 11 Democratic-Republican societies.

    B. The theorist of the Democratic-Republicans was John Taylor of Caroline.

        1. Taylor was an agrarian with no use for Hamilton's economics.

        2. Taylor blamed Hamilton for making parties necessary in *A Definition of Parties, or the Political Effect of the Paper System Considered* (1794).

    C. Hamilton began organizing himself under the name *Federalist.*

        1. He recruited Rufus King and Fisher Ames as congressional leaders.

        2. He established Federalist newspapers.

        3. Most Federalist support was in the urban seaports and depended on the national veneration of Washington.

III. The Republicans were nearly wrecked at the outset by their association with the excesses of the French Revolution.

    A. Jefferson was tenacious in his faith in the French Republic, but the revolution embarrassed the Republicans more and more.

        1. Ministers preached against the revolution as anti-Christ.

        2. The French Republic's minister, Edmond Genet, outraged Washington.

    B. Nevertheless, the Federalists managed to fumble away all these advantages.

        1. Hamilton could formulate policy but could not make it work.

> **2.** The Whiskey Rebellion made Hamilton and Washington appear heavy-handed.
>
> **3.** The Jay Treaty was so lopsidedly pro-British that the Federalist administration was embarrassed.

C. The 1796 election was won by Adams and the Federalists.

> **1.** However, under the Constitution's election procedures, Jefferson was elected vice president.
>
> **2.** Jefferson would use the vice presidency to frustrate Adams and the Federalists.

Essential Reading:

Jefferson, "Notes on the State of Virginia," in Peterson, *The Portable Thomas Jefferson*.

Supplementary Reading:

Joyce Appleby, *Capitalism and a New Social Order*.

Lance Banning, *The Jeffersonian Persuasion*.

Questions to Consider:

1. Why did the Constitutional Convention miss so completely the likelihood that political parties would develop in the new republic?

2. Were there any points of shared values between Republicans and Federalists?

Lecture Sixteen—Transcript
Republicans and Federalists

If there was one thing that Alexander Hamilton's argument for the Bank of the United States demonstrated, it was that the Constitution, while it was comprehensive, was not designed to anticipate every detail. The most unforeseen detail of them all, the one in fact that the creators of the Constitution would likely have outlawed if they had foreseen it in 1787, was the formation of political parties.

Until the 1790s, American politics was dominated, not by the politics of *party*, but by the politics of faction, or to use some of the other popular terms, "hunta," or "caucus." There were some significant differences between these two categories. Parties differ from factions in that, first of all, faction politics tends to be temporary. It forms around one or two issues, and then dissolves with the achievement of one or two political goals.

Parties, by contrast, are built around comprehensive, long-term formulas for public policy. Also, faction politics is generally local or regional or special interest oriented. Parties organize constituencies across the nation, and across class or ethnic lines. Also, faction politics is small scale; it usually pays little attention to the actual mechanics of obtaining support or recruiting political power. Usually, that's because factions are confident that the righteousness of their ideas is all they need, or because they're simply less interested in generating mass support than in influencing the results of one or two decisions. Parties, however, develop large-scale structures for nominations, for mass mobilizations of voters, for propaganda, and for charismatic symbols.

Faction politics, to come back to factions again, is also usually personal. It usually revolves around the personality of one or two important leaders, whereas parties offer more democratic structures for participation; more people can enter into the life of a party, and parties survive the loss or the defeat of their leaders. Their leaders might be defeated in an election, or in some form of political contest, but the party goes on. A faction might not.

All of these characteristics of the modern party system, without exception, stuck about as deeply in the craw of the idea of a republic, as the idea of hereditary monarchy, itself, in the 18th century. The reasons for the 18th-century republican revolution against parties is not difficult to see, because the nature of party politics cuts straight across the grain of what 18th-century Whig, republican writers thought of as the three touchstones of true republican politics; those three touchstones were liberty, virtue, and commerce—above all, virtue. Republics, precisely because they were no longer bound together the way monarchies were—by the potent and corrupt forces of hierarchy, kinship, and patronage—were fragile in nature. They didn't have the glue of corruption to hold them together. What they required to survive was a single virtuous mind and a single virtuous political order.

Now, parties are the very embodiment of ambition, of selfishness, and the most dreaded of all republican diseases, corruption. And so, republicans, in the 18th-century sense of the term, believed that parties were examples of the past that needed to be put down if a republic was to survive. "If I could not go to heaven, but with a party," Jefferson remarked, "I would not go at all." "Nothing could be more ill-judged," agreed Alexander Hamilton, in the first of *The Federalist Papers*, "than that intolerant spirit which has at all times characterized political parties."

As James Madison argued in the tenth of *The Federalist Papers*, "The whole purpose of the Constitution had been to prevent the divisions of party interest from corrupting the new republic, this elaborate system of electing a two-house Congress, with each having power to restrain the other's legislation."

That whole system was intended to weed out the unvirtuous and the self-interested, as it was put, "Men of factious tempers or local prejudices or of sinister designs." Instead, the process was intended to put the wisest and the least partisan individuals in control of the nation's destiny. What no one had counted on when the Constitution was written, however, was the seriousness of the split that opened up between Thomas Jefferson and Alexander Hamilton over policies and programs.

By 1791, that split was descending from the level of politics and programs to that of ideology. At that point, matters were beginning to take on the shape, not of faction politics, but of national party organization. No one of course, actually, deliberately set out to depart from the official republican pose of Whig non-partisanship. The parties, which eventually organized around Jefferson and Hamilton, denied that they were parties at all, and each claimed that it was simply giving voice to the great, virtuous republican consensus of the nation, and that it had to organize itself to do so, because of what the other side was doing. The other side committed the sin of party organization first. The other side forced we innocent, political bystanders to create a counter party in order to stamp out the corruption of the aggressors, the other guys.

As early as January of 1791, Jefferson was sneering that Hamilton was constructing a sect in the government, which was plainly biased toward monarchy and stock jobbers and king jobbers. The only solution was an act of organizational self-defense. "The only corrective of what is corrupt in our present trend of government," Jefferson wrote, "is the augmentation of the numbers of the lower house so as to get a more agricultural representation which may put that interest above that of the stock jobbers."

It was not Jefferson, however, but Madison who became the real organizer of what soon was known as the *Democratic-Republicans*, or more simply the Republicans. Born in 1751, Madison was a life-long friend of Thomas Jefferson's. Madison had been one of the principal architects of the federal Constitution, at the Constitutional Convention in Philadelphia in the summer of 1787. In the convention, Madison had allied himself with Hamilton during the debates in the states over the ratification of the Constitution. He added his voice to Hamilton and John Jay in creating *The Federalist Papers* in 1788. As a Virginian, as a slaveholder, and a gentleman farmer like Jefferson, though, he disagreed strongly with the direction Hamilton was setting in his reports. From his seat in the House of Representatives, Madison began to orchestrate an organized opposition to Hamilton in both the House and the Senate.

By October of 1791, Madison and Jefferson had expanded their congressional organization to include propaganda organs; sponsoring the publication of anti-Hamilton newspapers like the *National Gazette* and the *Philadelphia Aurora*, and anti-Hamilton editors like the wild-eyed Philip Freneau and Benjamin Franklin Bache, the grandson of Benjamin Franklin. What Madison accomplished as a Republican organizer in the Capitol, John Beckley, who was the clerk of the House of Representatives, accomplished on the local level.

A natural-born political manipulator, Beckley managed local Republican campaigns for office in Pennsylvania, distributed handbills and broadsides, and employed express riders to distribute ballots. In other words, he was doing pretty much the same thing as voter registration drives do today. He used family and kinship networks to get out the vote. By the time Jefferson left the cabinet at the end of 1793, anti-Hamilton societies were springing up on the local level all across the republic. Eleven clubs known as Democratic Societies, or Republican Societies, were in existence by the end of 1793. In the next year, another two dozen were organized in all but one of the states. Most of this grassroots organizing was based on an appeal to agricultural interests. This was suspicious to old anti-Federalists in the state governments and legislatures, who were still, even at this point, largely unreconciled to the Constitution. In the person of John Taylor of Caroline, the Republicans found an amateur political theorist who was capable of giving the Republicans a comprehensive political ideology that could articulate agricultural grievances in ways that the gangly Thomas Jefferson could not. John Taylor had no use for Hamilton's economics. The only result of Hamilton's policies, warned Taylor, "would be a peasantry wretchedly poor and an aristocracy luxuriously rich and arrogantly proud."

Now, by aristocracy, Taylor meant this legal faction of capitalists that Hamilton was promoting, an aristocracy of paper and patronage. As for the crime of creating a party, Taylor weighed in against Hamilton in his fat political tract, *A Definition of Parties: Or the Political Effects of the Paper System Considered*. In that, Taylor blamed Hamilton for making parties necessary. The people had no other recourse against Hamilton's corruptions except party organization. Now, one might as well admit the usefulness of party. "The existence of two parties in Congress is apparent," Taylor shrugged. "The fact is disclosed almost upon every important question."

Hamilton was clearly dismayed at the emergence of an organized party opposition. "This is the first symptom of a spirit which must either be killed or it will kill the Constitution," Hamilton complained. In August of 1792, he accused Madison and Jefferson of conspiracy against the administration—Madison for the expectation of popularity, and Jefferson because "Mr. Jefferson aims with ardent desire at the presidential chair."

The very existence of Philip Freneau's *National Gazette* as a party newspaper drove Hamilton wild. "The whole complexion of his paper is an exact copy of that patronage under which he acts. He is the faithful and devoted servant of the head of a party from whose hand he receives the boon." What drove Hamilton wilder still, was Jefferson's campaign to undermine Hamilton's own political base in New York, by recruiting two of the most important upstate New York politicians—George Clinton and Aaron Burr—to the Republican cause. Thus, in short order, Hamilton's rage at Jefferson's party organization turned him toward party organizing of his own.

Borrowing the name *Federalist* from the papers he had written in defense of the Constitution, Hamilton recruited his own cadre of congressional supporters, led by Rufus King of New York in the Senate, and Fisher Ames of Massachusetts in the House. Hamilton also used the backing of Washington to manage legislative timetables, conferences, and committee appointments, and to raise funds to establish Federalist newspapers, beginning with John Fenno's *Gazette of the United States*.

To a large extent, Hamilton did succeed in bending Congress to his will. Between 1789 and 1791, twice as many representatives in the House voted to support Hamilton's initiatives as those against. Hamilton did little of the grassroots organizing that the Republicans had done with their clubs and societies, though. Hamilton still had difficulty freeing himself from the notion that in a republic, politics should be non-partisan, should be virtuous and disinterested; the effect was that the only effective organization the Federalists really enjoyed was the one they managed to create inside Congress itself. Most of the popular support the Federalists enjoyed was either based in the great seaports of New England, New York, Philadelphia, Baltimore, Charleston, or else it was wrapped up in the national veneration for the figure of President Washington.

Now, take it all together and this does not look like a very well spread or well-organized base of political support. As events would prove, it wasn't. In 1795, though, the prestige of George Washington was worth the president's weight in gold. What was more, the Jeffersonian Republicans nearly destroyed themselves at the beginning by a catastrophic failure of political judgment.

Ten weeks after Washington's inauguration as the first president, in New York City, the starving mobs in the streets of Paris rose up and destroyed the Bastille—a one time prison and part-time arsenal in a working-class district of Paris. The fall of the Bastille became the emotional symbol of the French Revolution. The old French monarchy was replaced three days later by a constitutional monarchy and a new, liberal Constitution.

Jefferson, who had been serving out the end of a spell as American ambassador to France when this revolt erupted, took up his duties as Washington's secretary of state, almost delirious with joy over the French situation. France, who had been America's oldest ally, America's help during the American Revolution, had now joined America in revolution, and perhaps, France would join the United States as a sister republic. It would be the coming thing. It would be the leading edge; France and America together, changing the world, bringing down monarchy and unfair and born privilege.

Hamilton, likewise, wrote that the news of the French Revolution filled him with the same passions he had felt in 1775, but by 1792, it was a different story. The French Revolution, unlike the American Revolution, had rapidly turned from an experiment in republican liberty and virtue into a bloody vendetta against the French monarchy, marked in 1793 by the emergence of Maximilien Robespierre, and the imposition of Robespierre's Reign of Terror. Thousands of enemies of the French Revolution were paraded to the guillotine. Christianity was to be replaced by a religion of reason.

When a republic was officially proclaimed in France in September of 1793, Hamilton snorted at it as an insult to the name of "republic." When the French went to war against Britain and the other European monarchies, Hamilton urged Washington not to allow the United States to be dragged into collaboration with the French. These urgings were lost on Thomas Jefferson and his Republicans, who preferred to overlook the excesses of the French Republic on the grounds that a revolution in favor of liberty requires the breaking of a few royal heads.

With every fresh sensation from France, Jefferson's tenacious faith in the French Revolution embarrassed his Republicans more and more. The first envoy of the French Republic, Edmond Genet, outraged Washington by commissioning British ships to attack British merchant vessels. Now, think of the consequences of this. If

American merchant vessels receive a commission from an agent of the French Republic to go out and privateer on the high seas, capture British ships, and then destroy them or seize them as prizes, who will be blamed for that? France, perhaps, but remember those were American ships. Will not the British government then, also, put the blame at the door of the United States? Will that not lead to renewal of war, when war is the last thing the United States needs to contemplate right now?

Even Jefferson finally admitted that citizen Genet, and this bloodthirsty government would sink the Republican interest if they did not abandon him. He was not far from wrong.

Feeling against Genet erupted in Richmond, New York City, New Jersey, Maryland, and Delaware. Washington eventually, angrily, demanded that the French Republic revoke Genet's credentials. Yet, even with the advantages the Federalists enjoyed in Hamilton's leadership, in Washington's support, in their control of Congress, in their wealthy and upwardly mobile urban support, and in the folly of Jefferson's association with the French, what is simply amazing is how the Federalists so quickly fumbled all these advantages away.

Hamilton's skill in formulating public policy did not always translate well into making policy work. For instance, Hamilton's determination to fund the nation's Revolutionary War debt led to those tariffs on imports that I described earlier, and also that steep excise tax on whiskey. Now, Hamilton may have looked at whiskey production as a luxury: "All right, we'll tax that, and no one should really get terribly embarrassed about it." On the agricultural frontier, however, whisky was an efficient and profitable way to produce a useful commodity out of surplus grain. Grain, after all, will not keep. It does not have a long shelf life, so to speak. However, when you take grain and distill it down into whiskey, there is something that can stay on the shelf for a long time, and what's more, be easily brought to market and traded for other goods. To tax whiskey then, was to lay a heavy burden on the back of farmers who turned their excess grain into whiskey.

In the summer of 1794, farmers in western Pennsylvania and in North Carolina fought back by the methods that they had perfected all too well during the Revolution: mobs, intimidation of the tax collectors, a convention in Pittsburgh, and sure enough, Committees of Correspondence. Hamilton and Washington immediately interpreted the disturbances as a test of the federal government's authority, an all-or-nothing crisis in which it must be determined whether the government can maintain itself.

Secretary of War Knox sounded the alarm for 12,000 militiamen to assemble at Carlisle, Pennsylvania. At the end of September, Hamilton and Washington donned uniforms and took personal command of these forces, and marched westward to suppress the Whiskey Rebellion. The result was a fiasco. The whiskey tax resistors had no army. They simply melted away back to their farms, and who could tell who was who?

Hamilton longed to hang someone as an example. He tried to hang Hugh Henry Breckinridge, a journalist in Pittsburgh, when he discovered that Breckinridge had failed to properly sign his oath of submission to the excise law. In the end, though, the whole dramatic scene had to be called off, and Hamilton and Washington returned to Philadelphia looking considerably the sillier.

The Whiskey Rebellion turned out to be only the beginning of the Federalists' sorrows. In 1795, Washington sent John Jay to Britain to negotiate a commercial treaty that would settle a number of loose ends left over from the end of the Revolutionary War. In these negotiations, the British could afford to deal from strength, and the treaty that Jay came back to the United States with was so lopsided in the privileges given to British merchants that it nearly failed to get Senate approval.

The Jay Treaty certainly did not get popular approval. Jay remarked that he could have traveled from Boston to Philadelphia by night with the light thrown from burning effigies of himself dangling along the road. Then in 1795, the Federalist leadership began to disintegrate. Hamilton left the cabinet, physically exhausted and also needing to return to his lucrative law practice in New York, in order to recoup the income he'd lost while serving the public. Then, in the summer of 1796, Washington announced that he would not seek a third term as president.

That announcement at once deprived the Federalists of their most potent political figurehead. Benjamin Franklin Bache's *Aurora* trumpeted happily that, "the name of Washington from this day, ceases to give currency to political inequity." The Republicans in Congress immediately agreed to nominate Thomas Jefferson for the presidency, with the New Yorker—Aaron Burr—as his vice presidential choice.

The Federalists, by contrast, were paralyzed. The most obvious Federalist nominee was Washington's vice president, John Adams, but Hamilton suspected Adams, and rightly, of being less than an enthusiastic supporter of Hamilton's own Federalist agenda. Hamilton urged that Thomas Pickney of South Carolina be nominated instead. Well, in the end the Federalists compromised by running Adams for the presidency, with Pickney as his vice president. As it turned out, they compromised just in time.

The voting at the end of 1796, gave Adams the presidency, but only barely. The Constitution did not provide for the direct election of the president by the people of the United States. Remember from the last lecture, that because of their mistrust of the passions of the common herd, the authors of the Constitution had instead made eligible, white male voters in the states vote for slates of electors, pledged to the various presidency candidates, who would then in turn, meet and cast their electoral votes in the electoral college, so that the president was elected really not by a majority of the people, but by a majority of the electors.

To make this process even more complicated, the Constitution had made no provision for pairing the president and vice president in the election process as we do today. Today, when we think of people running for high office, we think of a ticket of president and vice president who are running together as a single unit. Well, that did not obtain under the Constitution originally. The Framers of the Constitution—who, of course, had never anticipated the emergence of political parties—had simply assumed that out of any group of likely and virtuous candidates for the presidency, the top vote getters would be the president, and the runner-up would be the vice president. Of course, by 1796, both Federalists and Republicans had taken on a political life of their own, and nominated their own choices for both president and vice president.

The "winner-take-all" process that the Constitution provided allowed for no distinction between a Federalist candidate for president, and a Republican nominee for vice president. The result was then that it was perfectly possible for the candidate of one party to garner the majority of votes and become president, while the runner-up might be the opposing party's candidate for president, thus saddling the president not with a vice president of his own choosing but with his erstwhile rival.

This, of course, is precisely what happened in the election of 1795. Adams squeaked into the Presidency with a total of 71 electoral votes, but his proposed vice presidential candidate—Pickney—picked up only 59 electoral votes. Thomas Jefferson, meanwhile, garnered 68 electoral votes, and by the law of the land, Thomas Jefferson, thereby, became John Adams's vice president. Jefferson also began a giant size cuckoo in the Federalists' political nest, for while Jefferson's powers as vice president would not be great, still the Constitution mandated that Jefferson would serve as the presiding officer of the Senate, and there was no doubt in anyone's mind but that he would use that position to frustrate every Federalist legislative initiative that appeared there.

Lecture Seventeen
Adams and Liberty

Scope:

Few people in the American republic genuinely liked John Adams. It was politically fortunate for Adams, then, that the first major challenge of his administration involved a foreign policy problem, where few Americans had more unchallenged expertise than he. It was even more politically fortunate that this crisis, the XYZ Affair, was provoked by the idol of the Democratic-Republicans, revolutionary France. Despite the fact that no actual declaration of war had been made, an undeclared quasi-war with France broke out on the high seas. But Adams squandered all the political capital he accumulated by backing the Alien and Sedition Acts and by abruptly entering into peace negotiations with the French. Hamilton attempted to persuade the Federalist Party to dump Adams before the election of 1800, but he only succeeded in dividing his own party and guaranteeing that the election would fall to Thomas Jefferson and the Democratic-Republicans.

Outline

I. Despite his long career of public service, John Adams was not well liked.

   A. His personal temperament was unattractive.

      1. Adams was vain and uncooperative.

      2. His *Defence of the Constitutions of Government of the United States* (1787) appeared to favor quasi-monarchy.

      3. At the same time, Adams showed no enthusiasm for Hamilton's economic program.

   B. Fortunately for Adams, his first challenge involved foreign policy.

      1. French ships at war with Britain were seizing American ships.

      2. Adams sent a three-man delegation—consisting of Pinckney, Marshall, and Gerry—to negotiate.

      3. They were met with demands for bribes.

      4. Adams released the news of the XYZ Affair to Congress and asked for military mobilization (1798).

      5. His particular triumph was the success of the American frigates.

II. But Adams proceeded to display the Federalist weakness for losing control.

    A. He created political martyrs out of the Republicans.

        1. In an effort to suppress French "sedition," Congress passed the Naturalization Act, the Act Concerning Aliens, the Act Concerning Alien Enemies, and the Sedition Act (the Alien and Sedition Acts) (1798).

        2. When the arrests centered on Republicans, public opinion swung against Adams.

        3. Jefferson and Madison drafted the Virginia and Kentucky resolutions, threatening nullification and secession.

    B. The French Directory was overthrown by Napoleon, ending the immediate threat of war with France.

        1. Adams unwisely opened negotiations with France and demobilized the military.

        2. Hamilton was so outraged that he inaugurated a dump-Adams movement in 1800.

        3. Hamilton split the Federalists, enabling Jefferson to capture the presidency and attempt the restoration of what he considered "true" republicanism.

Essential Reading:

Joseph J. Ellis, *American Sphinx: The Character of Thomas Jefferson*.

Supplementary Reading:

Lance Banning, *The Sacred Fire of Liberty*, chapter 7.

David G. McCullough, *John Adams*.

Questions to Consider:

1. Could Adams have used the opportunity of war with France to solidify the Federalist grip on political power?

2. Were the Virginia and Kentucky Resolutions an appropriate response to the Alien and Sedition Acts?

Lecture Seventeen—Transcript
Adams and Liberty

Few people in the American republic in the 1790s had a more distinguished record of public service than the second president of the United States, John Adams. Born and bred in Quincy, Massachusetts, Adams had spoken first for American liberty back in 1765 by denouncing the Stamp Act, and he had served in the Continental Congress from 1774 until 1778; he was the seconder of Richard Henry Lee's famous "Resolution for Independence," and then he served as a negotiator in London for the treaty that ended the American Revolution. He crowned that record of service by serving for four years as the first American ambassador to Great Britain, actually an American minister, to use the technical term, and for eight years he served as George Washington's vice president.

Yet, for all of that, few people in the American republic genuinely liked John Adams. He was 61 years old at the time of his election to the presidency in 1796. He was short, he was paunchy, he was temperamental, and he was not a little vain. He was the horror of Jefferson's Republicans for comments that he unloaded in a book he published in 1787, *Defence of the Constitutions of Government of the United States*, where he proposed that the old Confederation government might benefit from the creation of a Senate composed of the rich, the well-born, and the able.

Hamilton, however, also mistrusted Adam's loyalty, or at least Adam's loyalty to the Federalist program that Hamilton had put in place, because Adam showed no particular enthusiasm for government regulation of the economy, for protection or encouragement of home manufacturing, or for the Bank of the United States, and Adams remained throughout his life the very same thing that Thomas Jefferson was, a country lawyer with a farm to manage.

In Hamilton's mind, Adams was at best a lukewarm Federalist who deserved careful watching. In fact, it could be said with some justice that the Federalists backed Adams for the presidency only because they had no real alternative. Hamilton could not afford to take time away from his law practice to make a bid for the presidency, nor was it really clear that Hamilton could have beaten Thomas Jefferson in a flat-out electoral race. Thus, it was more by default than by decision that Adams became the Federalist nominee in 1796, and under those terms the results pretty well could have been predicted. Adams barely scraped into office, with lackluster Federalist support.

Every indication spelled contention and conflict for Adams and his divided, suspicious, and unenthusiastic party. The Federalist leader in the House of Representatives—Fisher Ames—was heard to moan, "I am ready to croak when I observe the gathering of vapors in our horizon." It was therefore politically fortunate for John Adams that the first major challenge of his administration involved a foreign policy problem—the area, of course, where few Americans had more unchallenged expertise than John Adams.

It was also even more politically fortunate that this crisis was provoked by the idol of the Jeffersonian Republicans, and that was France. By 1796, the French Revolution had blown out most of its own energies. The Reign of Terror that had so appalled sympathetic Americans in 1794 had collapsed in the reaction of Thermidor, and now France was governed by a five-man French Directory struggling to put the battered French Republic back on its feet.

It didn't help matters for the French Directory that France was still embroiled in a major war against the anti-revolutionary coalition of Austria, Prussia, Spain, and Great Britain, and for that reason the French expected, at the very least, the sympathy of the American republic, and at best, the trade and financial support of the Americans.

It got neither one nor the other, even if the American republic had been unanimous in its admiration for the French Directory, which it was not. American trade on the high seas was pitifully vulnerable to the naval power of France's great adversary, the British.

The British were quite well aware of this, and in December 1794, the British began seizing American ships caught trading in the Caribbean islands of the French West Indies, the presumption being that they were there to aid the French.

President Washington, who preferred restraint to a suicidal renewal of war with the British, chose to try negotiating with the British, and the result was the humiliation of the Jay Treaty, which we talked about last time. The Jay Treaty may have been the best the Americans could have obtained from the British, because the British were dealing from a position of unquestioned strength, but when the French Directory read the terms of the Jay Treaty, they immediately leapt to the conclusion that the Americans had sold them out. The French responded by declaring their own open season on American shipping in the war zones, hoping that a display of force from the French Navy would pressure the Americans into renouncing the Jay Treaty and resuming unrestricted trade with the French Directory. By the end of 1796, French seizures of American shipping in the Caribbean and the Mediterranean had reached almost the same proportions as the earlier British seizures of American shipping in the Caribbean.

This was the situation that greeted John Adams as soon as he had taken the Oath of Office in March of 1797, and he immediately called for a special session of Congress to deal with it. Adams was ready for war, but like Washington he resolved to try negotiation first, and in July of 1797, Adams dispatched a three-man commission: Charles Cotesworth Pinckney, John Marshall, and the Massachusetts Republican Elbridge Gerry. They were to meet in France with the leadership of the French Directory.

This time, however, the results of negotiation were fruitless. Kept waiting for weeks to see the French Directors, they were only at last admitted to a resultless interview with the wily French foreign minister, and incidentally turncoat aristocrat—Charles Maurice de Talleyrand. Afterwards, three of Talleyrand's agents approached the American commissioners and frankly suggested that the path of negotiation would become instantly and remarkably smoother if the Americans would make an immediate payment of about 240,000 dollars to Talleyrand. In other words, they were to put up a bribe, and then they would agree to guarantee loans of 10 million dollars to the French Directory as atonement for the Jay Treaty.

"It is no, no, not a sixpence," Commissioner Pinckney erupted in rage, and after six weeks of further waiting, the commissioners announced their departure and demanded their passports. President Adams received his first reports about the unhappy results of the negotiations in March of 1798, and shortly thereafter he sent a summary of them to Congress, but the summary deliberately left out the most inflammatory parts. Not until April, when Adams was sure that the commissioners were safely out of France, did Adams reveal the whole story of Talleyrand, and Talleyrand's extortion attempt, in a closed-door session of Congress. Even then, Adams declined to reveal the names of the French officials involved; he substituted for their names the letters X, Y, and Z.

Even so, the impact of this was staggering. Three days later, Adams released the full dispatches concerning the XYZ Affair to the Federalist newspapers, and the public uproar was awesome. Adams, for really the first time in his life, was hailed in song. Pinckney's defiant words were re-published as the even more defiant slogan, "Millions for defense, but not one cent for tribute."

Congress abrogated all treaties with France, dating all the way back to the French Alliance during the Revolution. In July, Congress authorized the seizure of any French ships that appeared to endanger American commerce, and authorized a national direct tax on property to raise two million dollars for bulking up the army and the navy.

Now, despite the fact that there had been no actual declaration of war, an undeclared naval war—the so-called quasi war with France—now broke out on the high seas. Nearly 80 French ships were gobbled up by the American Navy. The frigate *Constellation*, under the command of Commodore Thomas Truxton, fought and captured the French frigate *L'Insurgent*, and beat another one, the *Vengeance*, into a helpless hulk. Meanwhile, an additional army of 12 regiments of infantry and six troops of dragoons—12,500 men in all—were authorized, and Washington was given command of them as Lieutenant General. To the consternation of Adams and Jefferson, Washington insisted on Hamilton being made his Major General.

While this war fever was sending Federalist loyalty and enthusiasm to all time highs, it sent the reputation of Jefferson's Republicans into near fatal arrest. Republicans were now attacked as French sympathizers, as "Jacobeans," after the title of the most dreaded and radical revolutionaries of the Reign of Terror. They were denounced as Democrats, "mobocrats," and all other kinds of rats.

Overnight, the Federalists became the champions of American rights, while the Republicans were stigmatized as the lackeys of a foreign power. Adams, who was used to appearing in public without receiving the slightest mark of attention, was now cheered in theaters as the eagle-eyed and undaunted Adams; if Adams and his Federalists had had as clear a view of political opportunity as they did of public virtue, then it's entirely possible that they might have exploited this situation to its fullest, and discredited and eliminated Jefferson and the political power of Jefferson's Republicans for good and for all.

In fact, Adams proceeded to display the same alarming Federalist weakness for pulling defeat out of the jaws of victory that had dogged the closing months of Washington's second term. Adams did so with two blundering decisions that managed to give back to the Republicans their reputation as the defenders of liberty, and to take away from the Federalists their advantage as the geniuses of foreign policy.

The first of these blunders was the blessing Adams and the Federalists gave to the Alien and Sedition Acts. The second was Adams's decision to reopen treaty negotiations with the French Directory. The height of the war scare in the summer of 1798 turned Americans against anything and everything French, and it did not take long before Federalist newspapers began raising the stakes of accusation by suggesting, none too coyly, that the Republicans' admiration for France made every Republican at best a potential tool of French policy, and at worst, a traitor ready to join an invading French Army whenever it hit the beaches of North America.

When Federalist Roger Griswald of Connecticut made a slighting remark on the floor of the House of Representatives on January 30, 1798, about the Revolutionary War record of the Vermont Republican Matthew Lyon, the hot tempered Lyon rose and spat in Griswald's face. Two weeks later, on February 15, Griswald responded by beating Lyon with a hickory cane.

War scare paranoia hit its peak in the summer of 1798, in Congress, in the form of a series of bills known as the Alien and Sedition Acts. These acts were really four separate bills introduced by the Federalists in an effort, as one of their sponsors Senator James Lloyd of Maryland wrote to Washington, "To enable us to lay our hands on traitors." The first of the Alien and Sedition Acts was the Naturalization Act. Naturalization, of course, is the process whereby an alien—someone from another country, but who is resident in the United States and wants to become a citizen of the United States—becomes a citizen. The Naturalization Act aimed to increase the amount of time that it would take for an alien to go through the process of becoming an American citizen. It expanded from five to

14 years the statutory length of residence that immigrants have to spend in the United States before they can be naturalized as citizens.

Now what was this intended to accomplish? Well, it was aimed pretty plainly at keeping political power for as long as possible out of the hands of people born in other countries, because it was presumed that people born in other countries, especially if they were born in France, would be presumably sympathetic to the Republicans. "Well, you don't want them to become citizens too quickly now do you? Because when they do, they'll vote for Jefferson and the Republicans, so you extend the period of naturalization, not just five years now but 14 years, and effectively you create a long period of disenfranchisement, so that Republicans cannot automatically count on having that foreign-born vote behind them."

Now, on the surface, ostensibly, what this was supposed to do was to interject an element of caution into the naturalization process. "After all these French revolutionaries, these French Republicans have demonstrated that they can be really dangerous, so let's not extend citizenship too quickly; let's be very careful, let's do all the 18th-century versions of a background check that we need to do, and then after 14 years if good behavior has been manifest, then that will be the appropriate time to accept, let us say, a French immigrant as a citizen."

Well, that was the surface logic, but as I've indicated already, the political logic underneath the surface was: "How can we continue to keep the Republicans struggling for votes?" That was the first of the Alien and Sedition Acts. This was followed by the Act Concerning Aliens, and the Act Concerning Alien Enemies.

Having made it more difficult for an alien, an immigrant, to become a citizen, these two bills gave the president sweeping powers to act against those who were still only immigrants by permitting their arrest and deportation, if they were suspected of treasonable or secret leanings. The bill's sponsor, Harrison Gray Otis, explained pretty candidly that his legislation was prompted by his desire that "we not wish to invite hordes of wild Irishmen, nor the turbulent and disorderly of all parts of the world to come here with a view to disturb our tranquility, after having succeeded in the overthrow of their own governments. So let immigrants be put on notice by these bills, that if they immigrate to the United States, they can be sent back at a moment's notice, by order of the president if there was a suspicion that they have been involved in treasonous or seditious activities," with the definition of "treasonous or seditious activities" floating somewhere in the blue.

The next of the Alien and Sedition Acts was the Sedition Act. This was a bill that turned its attention not to aliens, not to immigrants, but to the native-born version of potential traitors. The Sedition Act established heavy fines and even imprisonment for writing, speaking, or publishing any false, scandalous, and malicious writings with intent to defame or to bring into contempt or disrepute the president or Congress. One supposes at this point that even someone who indulged in political humor—making a joke about how short, how fat, how bald John Adams was—might well find themselves falling under the ban of the Sedition Act.

It didn't take very long to discover who the most likely targets of the bills would be. Matthew Lyon, for instance, was arrested under the terms of the Sedition Act when his *Vermont Journal* recommended that John Adams be committed to a madhouse. Thomas Jefferson's favorite editor—the Irish-born William Duane—was indicted for seditious libel in Philadelphia. The indictment was overturned, only to be reinstated again in July of 1799, and then quashed again by a Senate committee.

Jedediah Peck was a Federalist Justice of the Peace from Otsego, New York, who despite being a Federalist still opposed the Alien and Sedition Acts as incredibly unwise. When he criticized the Acts, he found himself—despite the fact that he was a good Federalist— indicted for seditious libel and hauled to New York City in chains.

All told, 25 people were arrested under the terms of the Alien and Sedition Acts, but instead of this silencing some potentially subversive Republican or French fifth column in the United States, all that these arrests did was to convince everyone who heard of them that John Adams and the Federalists had simply gone over the top.

Arrests and trials under the Acts were turned into anti-Federalist carnivals. The Philadelphia jury that quashed William Duane's first indictment took less than half an hour to deliberate, and their verdict was greeted with cheers.

When Judge Peck was brought manacled and dragged from his home to New York City, his journey turned into what you can only call a martyr's progress. Listen to one description of this, "A hundred missionaries in the cause of democracy," here meaning not democracy as a political theory, but the Democratic-Republican Party of Jefferson, "stationed between New York and Cooperstown could not have done so much for the Republican cause as this journey of Judge Peck, as a prisoner from Otsego to the capital of the state. It was nothing less than the public exhibition of a suffering martyr for the freedom of speech and the press, and the right of petitioning to the view of the citizens of the various places through which the marshal traveled with his prisoner."

By the end of the year, Thomas Jefferson and James Madison had secretly drafted their own responses to the Alien and Sedition Acts, drawn up in the form of resolutions and adopted anonymously by the Republican-dominated state legislatures of Kentucky and Virginia in November and December of 1798. These Virginia and Kentucky Resolutions were able to publicly criticize Adams and the Alien and Sedition Acts without much likelihood that either of the legislatures or the anonymous authors were going to be arrested for their efforts. I mean, it was one thing if an individual French immigrant made some snappy comment about John Adams, but when the entire legislature of Kentucky, or the entire legislature of Virginia has something to say on the subject it's going to be a little difficult to indict all of them.

Both the Virginia and Kentucky Resolutions ringingly invoked hallowed republican principles to denounce the Alien and Sedition Acts: "The liberty of conscience and of the press cannot be cancelled, abridged, restrained, or modified by any authority of the United States. Consequently," declared Madison, "the Sedition Act ought to arouse universal alarm, because it is leveled against the right of freely examining public characters and public measures—it's aimed at free communication among the people, which has ever been justly deemed the only effectual guardian of every other right. Let these Acts stand."

This is what both sets of resolutions warned: "Let these Acts stand, that it might be necessary for the individual states of the Union to assert the powers they possessed under the Tenth Amendment," the very same powers that Thomas Jefferson was convinced Hamilton had abused in creating the Bank of the United States, "and then the states would declare these Acts void and of no force."

In other words, states would take it upon themselves to nullify federal legislation, and Madison hinted even more darkly that the ultimate remedy might have to be the secession of states from the Federal Union, "since as Virginians," said Madison, "we're determined to sever ourselves from that Union we so much value rather than give up the rights to self government which we have reserved." Jefferson and Madison called upon the legislatures of the other states to endorse these resolutions. To their disappointment, none did, and in fact the Federalists in Congress quashed attempts in the fall of 1798 to get the Acts repealed.

Jefferson was not discouraged by this, though, and in fact he saw the in the long view where this eventually was bound to go. In 1798, he was actually more optimistic about the Republican future than at any time since he had left Washington's cabinet. "The frenzy over the quasi war with France would abate," Jefferson predicted, "and with a little patience we shall see the reign of witches pass over, their spells dissolved, and the people recovering their true sight—restoring their government to its true principles."

Just as if it was done on cue, the French menace that had been the original rationale for the Alien and Sedition Acts promptly proceeded to disappear. The armies of the French Directory, now commanded by an upstart named Napoleon Bonaparte, had sailed off to Egypt in the summer of 1798 to cut the British lifeline to India. In the process, the British Navy caught the French fleet napping at Aboukir Bay on August 1 and annihilated it, thus effectively ending the French naval threat to American ships.

From then on, the French Directory was on the road to collapse, and collapse it finally did in November of 1799, when Bonaparte seized power in a massive *coup d'etat*. With the threat of French invasion subsiding, so did the fears of subversion at home, and suddenly, by February of 1799, Congress found itself inundated with petitions demanding the repeal of the Alien and Sedition Acts, and the demobilization of the additional army.

Only a renewed demand for war, based upon a new war scare, could have saved the Federalists at this point. Perhaps some other Federalist president might have manufactured just such a crisis, but at this point President Adams stepped in and announced that he intended to reopen the failed negotiations with France; it was a very statesmanlike gesture. It outraged his fellow Federalists, however;

they saw Adams as simultaneously negotiating with the revolutionary great Satan, France, declaring public indulgence for Jacobean principles at home, and perhaps worst of all, bargaining away his party's one major political asset.

No Federalist was more furious over Adams's conduct than Alexander Hamilton, and it was Hamilton who attempted to mount a dump-Adams campaign in the spring of 1800, in order to replace Adams on the Federalist ticket for the presidential election that fall. Despite the knowledge that the Republicans would once again run Thomas Jefferson, and that only absolute party unity behind Adams could hope to turn Jefferson back, Hamilton obstructed Adams's reelection campaign at every turn. Sure enough, in the fall of 1800, when Jefferson and the Republicans once more challenged Adams and the Federalists, the divided and distracted Federalists crashed.

Jefferson and his vice presidential nominee, the New Yorker, Aaron Burr, polled 73 electoral votes, while Adams gathered only 65 electoral votes. For all practical purposes, the Federalist era was over, and the Federalist Party was effectively finished as a political force everywhere except in New England. Meanwhile, Thomas Jefferson and his Republicans now prepared to step forward, and brush aside the 12 years of Federalist rule as a great mistake, as a temporary hallucination, and then proceed to reorganize the nation on what Jefferson regarded as the "true" principles of virtuous republicanism.

Lecture Eighteen
The Jeffersonian Reaction

Scope:

There was no question in Thomas Jefferson's mind but that Hamilton and Adams had betrayed the original spirit of the American Revolution. He would dismantle the structure of the federal government, contain the size of the military, and show no favoritism in foreign policy or trade. But Jefferson was not nearly the radical that his enemies and friends alike painted him to be, nor was he politically skilled. He was utterly incapable of creating a practical set of alternatives to Hamilton's hard-headed fiscal policies. He had no sooner demobilized the navy than a war with the pirates of the North African (Barbary) coast broke out. And his solution to keeping America out of the quarrel between Great Britain and revolutionary France was to impose a sweeping export embargo that did nothing to hurt the British or the French but nearly bankrupted the American economy. He was also taken by surprise by the emerging activism of the federal judiciary, which under Chief Justice John Marshall, began to operate as a serious restraint on the scope of Jefferson's actions (*Marbury v. Madison, Martin v. Hunter's Lessee, McCulloch v. Maryland*).

Outline

I. Thomas Jefferson looked on his election as a new start for American republicanism.

    A. He was convinced that Hamilton and the Federalists had betrayed republicanism.

        1. The Federalists' opposition to the French Revolution was evidence of common cause with Britain.

        2. Hamilton's reports were evidence of a determination to entangle America in British finance.

    B. Jefferson was determined to do away with Federalist influence.

        1. His inauguration was the first to be held in Washington, free from corrupting influences in Philadelphia.

        2. He would dismantle the structure of federal government.

3. He would contain the size of the military.

4. There would be no favoritism in foreign policy.

II. However, Jefferson's administration turned out not to be as radical as it at first seemed.

   A. Jefferson made no effort to extend voting rights.

      1. In many states, voting rights were actually decreased.

      2. Jefferson's only solution was to increase property-holding.

   B. Jefferson was not successful in promoting an agrarian agenda.

      1. He personally knew little about agriculture.

      2. He had no objection against small-scale manufacturing.

   C. Jefferson was an ineffective administrator.

      1. He failed to displace Hamilton's fiscal policies.

      2. He canceled military spending, only to be embarrassed by the Barbary pirates (1801–1804).

   D. Jefferson attempted to solve the problem of British and French depredations on American commerce with a national embargo on exports.

      1. Renewal of war between France and Great Britain in 1803 made American ships sitting ducks.

      2. A British frigate, *Leopard*, assaulted an American frigate, *Chesapeake*, in 1807.

      3. Jefferson called for an embargo in 1808 to force the British and French to cave in.

      4. Instead, the embargo beggared the American economy.

   E. Jefferson was hamstrung by the federal courts.

      1. John Marshall was one of Adams's last appointments, as chief justice of the U.S. Supreme Court.

      2. He successfully choked off the application of Jefferson's "revolution of 1800" through Court decisions.

         a. *Marbury v. Madison* (1803) established the principle of judicial review.

         b. *Martin v. Hunter's Lessee* established the authority of the federal courts over the state courts.

         c. *McCulloch v. Maryland* argued for the existence of "implied powers" in the federal government.

Essential Reading:

Charles S. Hyneman and Donald Lutz, eds., *American Political Writings during the Founding Era, 1760–1805*, vol. 2, documents 67–76.

Supplementary Reading:

R. Kent Newmyer, *John Marshall and the Heroic Age of the Supreme Court*.

G. Edward White, *The Marshall Court and Cultural Change*.

Questions to Consider:

1. Do you believe the kind of Court that Marshall created was what the Constitution originally envisioned in providing for a Supreme Court?

2. In what ways are the Marshall decisions still important today?

Lecture Eighteen—Transcript
The Jeffersonian Reaction

There was no question in Thomas Jefferson's mind but that his election as the third President of the United States meant a completely new start for the practice of American republicanism. Through the 1790s, Jefferson had gradually convinced himself that Hamilton and Adams had betrayed the original spirit of republicanism, even to the point of selling the American republic back into the hands of the British and the British aristocracy. As it was, this new presidency, this "revolution of 1800," as Jefferson liked to call his election, would, as he promised, prove to be as real a revolution in the principles of our government as that of 1776 was in its form.

Certainly, everything about his inauguration on March 4, 1801, seemed to point to a dramatic new departure in American republicanism. For one thing, it was the first inauguration to take place in the new federal city of Washington and, as if to underscore the new beginning that his inauguration would bring, Jefferson deliberately laid aside the formal flourishes: the silver-buckle shoes, the knee britches and wigs, the swords—which all been the staple of Federalist public dress—and instead, he walked to the Capitol, accompanied by only a few friends and officials and a company of Maryland militia.

His inaugural address laid out the course he intended to take with unmistakable clarity. First of all, he would dismantle the structure of federal government built up by Hamilton, and pay off the national indebtedness that had made taxation and the Bank of the United States necessary. The second thing he would do would be to contain the size of the military, because permanent military forces were always a threat to the independence of a republic and, of course, military forces had been identified with Washington and with Hamilton.

Thirdly, Jefferson laid out, there would be no favoritism shown in foreign policy. What that meant, translated, was that there would be no concessions to the British, who were still at war with the French. Linked to that, Jefferson announced that he would support free trade and free commerce, which meant that there would be an end to the Hamiltonian tariffs that kept foreign manufactured goods at artificially high prices for farmers in order to benefit American manufacturers.

One other thing: Jefferson promised that he would deal gently with his Federalist opponents. This was, in fact, a great moment in the history of political systems, because it is one of those rare moments when a party, or an individual, possessing power, speaking for the majority, agrees that that power will not be used by the majority to take revenge on the minority, and the minority agrees in effect to be a minority, to recognize that it has lost, but not on that basis to attempt to disrupt or overturn the system.

The smooth transition of power between these two very dissimilar leaders, Adams and Jefferson, was a real watershed. It showed that a republican experiment in popular government, even when opinion in that government was divided, could in fact take place, and that republics could survive. But, as much as he would deal gently with the Federalists, he also made it clear that he would deal firmly with them.

In his inaugural address, Jefferson extended what sounded very much like an olive branch. "We have called by different names, brethren of the same principles. We are all Republicans. We are all Federalists." On the one hand, Jefferson was reaching out a hand of cooperation to the Federalists and saying, "No matter what our divisions, we really are all on the same team." However, what he meant by that was that everyone should join his team and abandon the rival team. What he meant was the elimination of the Federalists, and indeed the elimination of all party spirit, that bane of republican virtue. The unhappy John Adams stayed up nights in the week before Jefferson's inauguration, busily signing commissions for Federalist judges, so that at least the courts could be kept out of Jefferson's claws, and he left Washington early on the morning of Inauguration Day, as much because he could not stand the thought of personally handing the government over to Jefferson as because no one among the victorious Republicans had thought to send him an invitation.

Yet, despite Jefferson's confident predictions about what he was going to do, and Adams's fears about what he was going to do, Jefferson turned out to be a far cry from some kind of American Robespierre. For one thing, Jefferson was not nearly the radical that his enemies painted him to be. A case in point concerns the most basic symbol of republican community, the right to vote. Nearly two thirds of the electors who made Jefferson president had been chosen by their state legislatures, and over the next 20 years of Jeffersonian Republican rule in Washington, while local legislatures extended voting rights to more and more white males between 1800 and 1820, those legislatures also took those rights away from others who had previously enjoyed voting rights.

In 1810, Maryland stripped free blacks of voting rights that they had enjoyed since before the Revolution. New York, Tennessee, and North Carolina all followed Maryland's lead, while in New Jersey in 1807, women also lost voting rights; with all of this Jefferson had little or no quarrel. Jefferson did not believe in universal voting rights. To the contrary, he wanted voting rights linked to property-holding, and for those who did not own property, well, his solution was not to give them the vote but to give them property. In fact, he urged Congress to divide up the public lands in the West among property-less male citizens at a rate of 50 acres apiece, and thus turn them all into the kind of independent farmers that he believed to be the backbone of republican virtue. Under Jefferson's notions of republicanism, the American republic actually grew less democratic than it had been under the Federalists. Under Jefferson's regime, all white men would be equal, but no one else would be the equal of white men.

Nor was Jefferson exactly the model of a perfectly virtuous farmer. Although he was trained as a lawyer, Jefferson never earned a meaningful living from the law after his 30th birthday, and he based his wealth and his standing in Virginia society on the lands he inherited from his father and his in-laws. He was an enlightened dabbler. He liked to experiment with gadgets; he invented a new plow. He designed his own home—Monticello—and he assembled a library of 6,500 volumes. That's more than many public libraries have today.

The actual work that earned him his bread, however, was done by a small army of black slaves whom he did not hesitate to sell when he needed cash, and whom he did not hesitate to track down when they ran away. Above all, Thomas Jefferson was not an enemy to all forms of commerce. He hesitated to give encouragement to large-scale manufacturing, because he feared that it concentrated too much power in one place, reduced too many people to the status of mere wage earners, and would have to be financed—or at least protected—by tariffs that would unfairly burden the agricultural sector but, on the other hand, he had no objection to small-scale manufacturing. Some small-scale household manufacturing was in fact needed to supplement agriculture.

Still, it was not Jefferson's inconsistencies as a Republican that guaranteed that his "revolution of 1800" would fall short of overturning the Hamiltonian agenda as it was one other major factor, and that was Jefferson's incompetence as a president. Although Thomas Jefferson had spent all of his life since 1774 in one form or other in public service, it was not his administrative gifts for which he was famous. He might be the author of the Declaration of Independence, he might be the Republicans' great figurehead, he might be one of the most gifted talkers and writers on the North American continent, but he was utterly incapable of creating a practical set of alternatives to Hamilton's hard-headed fiscal policies.

Jefferson, for instance, struggled from the very first to pay off the national debt and cancel the taxes Hamilton had imposed for funding the debt and, by scrimping and saving, Jefferson actually succeeded in reducing the national debt from 83 million dollars to 57 million dollars over the course of his two terms of office, but doing more than that proved to be utterly beyond him. Even though Jefferson enjoyed a commanding margin of support in the House of Representatives, because there the Republicans had won 66 of the 106 seats in the House, and even though he had a working majority in the Senate, Jefferson still feared what would happen if he attempted to reverse Hamilton's plans and repudiate the debt outright.

Jefferson also hesitated to tamper with the Bank of the United States. As he confessed to his own very talented secretary of the treasury, Albert Gallatin: "It might be just as well to let the bank live," in order to demonstrate that the Republicans were not the enemies of commerce, and so, as Jefferson put it, "Detach the mercantile interest from its enemies," or, in this case, Jefferson's enemies "and incorporate them into the body of its friends."

Jefferson's greatest problem in dealing with the Hamiltonian agenda was his own inability to figure out where to begin demolishing it without bringing down the entire American economy, though. "We can never get rid of his financial system," Jefferson moaned. "It mortifies me to be strengthening principles which I deem radically vicious, but this vice is entailed upon us by the first error." One area of finance that Jefferson could deal with directly as the executive was the military, and true to his promises, he cashiered all of the army except for 3,000 regulars and 172 officers. He also canceled the remaining program of ship construction that Adams had authorized for the navy during the quasi war with France, and he ordered the half dozen or so frigates of the American Navy laid up in favor of building a flotilla of coast-defense gunboats. No sooner had he done so than the Pasha of Tripoli made him regret it.

The Pasha of Tripoli was a pirate. He was the ruler of one of the many Islamic private kingdoms on the North African coastline or, as it was known then, the Barbary Coast, from the Arabic term for North African Arabs, Berbers. The North African coast and the pirates who inhabited it were a nuisance to everyone's shipping in the Mediterranean, but most countries, including the United States, found it less expensive to bribe the pirates to stay away from their shipping rather than to mount an expensive expedition to clean out their North African nests. In May of 1801, however, the Pasha of Tripoli, noticing the defenseless condition of American merchant shipping, upped the ante of his annual payoff from the United States.

Rather than tax his virtuous Virginia farmers for tribute to pay to the Pasha of Tripoli, Jefferson uncharacteristically decided that he was going to spend the money on war. The frigates were hauled back into commission, and Jefferson sent them to the Mediterranean to deal with the pirates. Ahh, easier said than done. The Barbary pirates proved to be a good deal wilier than the American Navy, and not until 1804 did the Americans finally bring the Pasha to the bargaining table. Even then he was paid $60,000 for an agreement to leave American ships alone.

Maybe the most difficult moment Jefferson faced, or shall we say the most difficult moment Jefferson created for himself in an effort to wiggle out from the grasp of Federalism, was based on his policy toward the French. For all of his admiration for the French Republic, Jefferson was under no illusions about how the fortunes of the French Revolution had spiraled downward after the Reign of Terror. The French Directory had not been his favorite form of government. He was not happy to see the French Republic go in that direction, and when the French Directory was overthrown by Napoleon

Bonaparte in 1799, Jefferson angrily denounced Bonaparte as "the great beast."

The great beast not only appalled Jefferson; he provoked a renewal of France's war with Britain and, in terms reminiscent of 1796, announced an absolute blockade of the British Isles. The British, who were now fighting for their lives without a single ally left, responded in 1806 with a counter-blockade, and caught in the middle once more between the French and the British were American merchant ships; once again, the American Merchant Marine became the sitting ducks of the North Atlantic.

Between 1803 and 1807, the British seized over 500 American ships; the French seized over 300. This time around, though, it was the British who came to blows with the American Navy. In June of 1807, the British frigate *Leopard* stopped the American frigate *Chesapeake* to demand the return of British deserters rumored to be among the American crew. The *Chesapeake*, which was actually at that point en route to the Mediterranean, was not cleared for battle. Nevertheless, she still refused the British demand, unable to believe that the British would turn to force, which they did. The *Leopard* opened fire on the *Chesapeake*, killing three Americans and wounding 18. The *Chesapeake*, unable to return the fire, was compelled to strike her colors. The British boarded her, and hauled off four sailors—three of them undeniably American citizens, and two of them were black.

The *Chesapeake* incident created a storm of outrage exceeding even that of the XYZ Affair, but Jefferson, through his own parsimony, had no fleet at hand with which to retaliate against the world's greatest naval power. The expedient he hit upon instead was a universal boycott. To protest the high-handedness of both Britain and France, the United States would break off all trade with both warring powers until they came to their senses and permitted American ships to trade freely once again. Jefferson was confident that both the French and the British were so dependent on American agricultural products that both would cave in at once, and even if they didn't, so what? Americans would simply keep their agricultural products for themselves and declare a pox on both their houses.

Thus, in December of 1807, an exasperated and overwhelmingly Republican Congress approved an Embargo Act and sat back to enjoy the results. As it turned out, the results were anything but enjoyable. American exports dropped from 108 million dollars in 1807 to 22 million dollars. Imports plunged from 138 million dollars to 57 million. Merchants in the American port cities went bankrupt, taking their banks down along with them in the process, and dockworkers and the trades that depended on them were flung into unemployment. Jefferson refused to admit that the embargo was a mistake but, by the end of his second term in 1808, he had for all practical purposes given up trying to enforce it. One of the great problems that Jefferson faced came, in fact, from within his own government, and that concerned the judicial system.

Like voting, like citizenship, the Constitution had specified little about the functions and purposes of the federal judicial system, but Hamilton, as early as the 78th of *The Federalist Papers*, had seen the judiciary as outlined in the Constitution as a useful ally in keeping the authority of the states in line. It was not Hamilton, however, who was to prove the usefulness of the courts in hamstringing Jefferson and the Republicans, but one of John Adams's last official appointments—John Marshall of Virginia. We have already met John Marshall in earlier lectures.

Marshall had served, like Alexander Hamilton, on Washington's staff, and again, like Hamilton, Marshall identified himself wholly with the interests of the new constitutional government rather than the states. Marshall served briefly in the House of Representatives, then filled the post of secretary of state under John Adams, and in the waning months of Adams's presidency, Adams appointed Marshall as chief justice of the U.S. Supreme Court.

Well, Marshall was not a legal theorist, but he was also not afraid to assert the powers of the judiciary if he thought it was necessary to preserve the republic from mad dog Jeffersonianism, and in three major decisions Marshall and his Court not only effectively choked off Jefferson's "revolution of 1800," but also laid the practical groundwork for the powers of the federal courts ever since. The first of these decisions is known as *Marbury v. Madison*. This was Marshall's first great decision, and in fact it was linked closely to his own appointment, and to all the other judicial appointments, made by President Adams in the last week of his presidency.

Adams might have signed judicial commissions right up to the last minute of the last midnight of his presidency, but when the Republicans discovered this, they angrily announced their intention to disregard such appointments in some cases. Jefferson's secretary of state, James Madison, actually refused to deliver the signed commissions of these last-minute judges. Well, one of these judges, William Marbury, promptly filed suit against Madison in federal court, asking for a writ of mandamus that would compel Madison to deliver the commission. I mean, Republicans might not have liked John Adams's choices for judges; they might not have liked the fact that Adams used the last week of his presidency to hurry up and sign them and put those new judges into office; they might not have been thinking that that was a good idea at all; and they might not have liked the process but, notwithstanding, it was still legal.

Marshall heard the case and handed down the Supreme Court's unanimous decision on February 24, 1803. It was a delicately worded little bombshell. On the one hand, Marshall was determined that it would be unwise to provoke Jefferson and the Republicans into an outright confrontation over these appointments, and so Marshall ruled that Marbury's application to the federal courts for redress was invalid on a technicality. The Supreme Court, Marshall insisted, was a court of appeals. Marbury should have filed his suit at a different level. On the other hand, Marshall warned, if Marbury had followed the proper procedures, then Madison's refusal to deliver the commission would have been illegal, and both Madison and Jefferson would have had to obey a decision of the court to deliver the commission.

By sugar-coating the pill with a denial on the grounds of procedure, Marshall forced Jefferson and the Republicans to concede the power of the Court to review actions of the presidency and actions of the Congress, and so the principle of judicial review of federal legislation and executive action was moved into the high Court's grasp.

The second of the Marshall Court's great decisions this way was *Martin v. Hunter's Lessee*. If *Marbury v. Madison* established the Supreme Court's jurisdiction over the acts of the federal government, then *Martin v. Hunter's Lessee* established its authority over the state courts. This case arose out of a suit brought after the Revolution by Denny Martin, the heir of a loyalist family whose Virginia lands had been confiscated by the revolutionaries and sold to one David Hunter. The Jay Treaty had granted protection to loyalist property, and on the strength of that provision and the federal Constitution's pledge that such treaties were part of the supreme law of the land; Martin sued Hunter in the Court of Appeals of Virginia.

Martin's suit was denied, and so he appealed to the Supreme Court for relief. The Supreme Court ruled in Martin's favor and instructed the Virginia court to restore title to the property to Martin. Virginia, and this was the argument of justice Joseph Storey, had surrendered the sovereignty of her courts to the United States upon ratifying the Constitution. Therefore, since the Jay Treaty was part of the supreme law of the land by the Constitution, the state courts of Virginia had no business and no authority to override what was now federal jurisdiction. Once again, the Marshall Court had clearly placed the authority of the federal government and especially the federal courts over that of any rivals.

The third great case in the Marshall Court's history of cases was *McCulloch v. Maryland*. *Marbury v. Madison* and *Martin v. Hunter's Lessee* were really exercises in constitutional jurisdiction. *McCulloch v. Maryland* was a practical challenge to Hamilton's most important economic institution, the Bank of the United States.

In 1816, the Republican-dominated legislature of Maryland, fearful of the financial power of the bank, attempted to break the bank's power in Maryland by imposing a stamp tax on the bank notes issued by the Bank of the United States's Baltimore office. By taxing the bank notes, Maryland hoped to make them so expensive that people would cease using them in Maryland, and thus drive the bank's influence entirely out of the state. However, the bank's Baltimore cashier, John McCulloch, refused to pay the state tax on the grounds that Maryland had no sovereignty over an agency of the federal government and, if you don't have sovereignty over something, you have no right to tax it.

Maryland thereupon sued McCulloch personally, and when the Maryland courts decided, not surprisingly, in Maryland's favor, the Bank of the United States appealed to the United States Supreme Court. *McCulloch v. Maryland* was argued for nine days before the Court, with Luther Martin, the Maryland Attorney General, reviving Jefferson's old claim that the chartering of the bank exceeded the enumerated powers of the federal government under the Constitution and was therefore an unconstitutional entity.

Three days after the close of argument, Marshall handed down the Court's decision in favor of the Bank of the United States, and in it Marshall destroyed not only Martin's argument about the enumerated powers, but also the pretended power of the states to make decisions about what qualified or did not qualify as constitutional powers, reviving Hamilton's old argument that the Constitution implied the award of certain unspecified powers to the federal government. Remember we said earlier: The philosophy that Hamilton operated under, and which he used to persuade Washington to sign part of the legislation that put his economic program in place, was the idea that if the Constitution specifies an end, then the means necessary to achieve that end must also be constitutional.

Well, Marshall picked up the same Hamiltonian logic, and he scolded Martin for expecting the specification of every detail of the means of government in its Constitution when the Constitution is specifying its ends. "After all," Marshall wrote, "we must never forget that it is a Constitution we are expounding, not a series of suggestions, not just a series of statutes which can be succeeded by other statutes as people wish. It is a Constitution, a foundational document." Each of these decisions left Thomas Jefferson and James Madison fuming over Marshall and the courts. It's no wonder, then, that a mortified Thomas Jefferson soon abandoned his frustrating struggle with finance, with taxes, with the British, with the Barbary pirates, with the embargo, with John Marshall, and turned his attention westward across the Mississippi, where he did not have to worry about dealing with the lively ghost of Alexander Hamilton.

Lecture Nineteen
Territory and Treason

Scope:

Nothing terrified the thinking of the American Republic in the first 30 years of its existence more than the fear that somehow, the United States would be ground to pieces between the conflicts of the great European powers and re-colonized. The entire western agricultural traffic along the Mississippi could be held hostage by whoever held New Orleans (at this point, Napoleon Bonaparte's French Empire). But with renewed war in Europe on the horizon, Napoleon needed cash more than he needed Louisiana; thus, in April of 1803, Napoleon offered to sell not only New Orleans, but all of the Louisiana province—approximately 830,000 square miles—for $15 million in spot cash. Because descriptions of the boundaries of Louisiana were deliberately vague, Jefferson asked Congress to finance a secret scouting party up the Missouri River valley to the Pacific in the spring of 1803 under Lewis and Clark. A different kind of exploration was conducted by former Vice President Aaron Burr, who attempted to set up his own independent republic in the Mississippi valley. But Burr's conspiracy fell apart, and he was saved from a treason indictment only by Chief Justice John Marshall.

Outline

I. Americans feared the threat to their independence from European empires.

    A. They feared military actions from the Europeans.

        1. Napoleon's armies toppled one European kingdom after another.

        2. The British responded by preemptive strikes against neutral powers.

        3. The British and French aggressively poached on American shipping in the West Indies.

    B. Americans also feared betrayal to the European empires from within.

        1. Jefferson accused the Federalists of pro-British treason (for example, the Jay Treaty).

2. Federalists were convinced that the Jeffersonians would plunge them into a pro-French proxy war against Great Britain.

C. Jefferson personally hoped to avoid any involvement with Europe by turning American attention westward, to ensure American self-sufficiency.
1. By 1800, the American population in the trans-Appalachia had grown by 400 percent.
2. Ohio was the first state to be organized from the Northwest Territory, in 1803.

D. The problem with westward expansion was that it oriented trade toward New Orleans, then in Spanish hands.
1. Bonaparte intended to make New Orleans the center of a plan to revive France's colonial empire in North America.
2. Bonaparte's plan failed because of the resistance of black San Domingue.
3. Bonaparte then offered to sell Louisiana to the United States, and Jefferson accepted.
4. Jefferson had already explored the Louisiana Territory by means of secret exploring parties under Lewis and Clark, Zebulon Pike, and commercial freelancers (John Jacob Astor).

II. Louisiana, however, also opened up opportunities for plotters.

A. The most sinister of these plotters was Aaron Burr.
1. Burr was the grandson of Jonathan Edwards and Jefferson's former vice president.
2. He goaded Alexander Hamilton into a fatal duel in 1804.

B. Burr plotted to set up an independent republic in Louisiana.
1. He offered to make the territory a British dependency.
2. He recruited General James Wilkinson to betray New Orleans.
3. Wilkinson subsequently double-crossed Burr, and Burr was arrested.

C. Burr's treason trial was a fiasco for Jefferson.
1. Burr had covered his tracks very effectively.
2. Chief Justice Marshall was eager to even scores with Jefferson.

3. Burr was acquitted, went into exile, and returned to the United States in 1812.

Essential Reading:

Mary Jo Kline, ed., *The Political Correspondence and Public Papers of Aaron Burr*, vol. 2.

Supplementary Reading:

Joseph J. Ellis, *Founding Brothers*.

Forrest McDonald, *The Presidency of Thomas Jefferson*.

Questions to Consider:

1. What might have been the results for the United States had Burr's conspiracy to create an independent republic in the Southwest succeeded?

2. In what ways were Jefferson's actions as president inconsistent with the Republican Party attitudes?

Lecture Nineteen—Transcript
Territory and Treason

Nothing terrified the thinking of the American Republic in the first 30 years of its existence more than the fear that somehow the United States would be ground to pieces between the conflicts of the great European powers and then re-colonized by one of them, or perhaps several of them. The fear of conquest and re-colonization was made even sharper by the accusations and counter-accusations of both Republicans and Federalists. Each accused the other of being only too willing to sell the United States back into colonial subjugation in order to further their own secret anti-Republican interests. Jefferson's Republicans, for instance, accused Hamilton and the Federalists of secret sympathies for British aristocracy. John Adams was particularly pointed out as having written political treatises that advocated monarchy. Well, not literally, but that was what he really meant, at least according to the Republicans.

On the other hand, Federalists like Fisher Ames were just as convinced that Jefferson's election as president in 1800 would lead nowhere except to war with Great Britain, a Cisalpine alliance with France, plunder and anarchy. Well, Jefferson attempted to calm those anxieties by denying any intention of linking American interests with any European power. Especially after Napoleon betrayed the Republican hopes of France by proclaiming himself Emperor of France in 1804, Jefferson declared his perfect hostility to any American involvement in European affairs—French, British, or what have you. "We have a perfect horror at everything, like connecting ourselves with the politics of Europe," he wrote in 1801. "We wish to let every treaty we have drop off without renewal. We call in our diplomatic missions, barely keeping up those to the most important nations."

It was the political equivalent of the embargo. These protests were not just a smokescreen to confuse the Federalist opposition, either. Jefferson was convinced that the survival of Republican principles depended on promoting American self-sufficiency, and especially a self-sufficient agricultural economy. That meant opening up the Republic's undeveloped western territories, which lay between the Appalachian Mountains and America's western boundary on the Mississippi River. There—and this is what he predicted in his inaugural address in 1801—Americans would find enough land to make everyone an independent land holder, enough to absorb 1,000 generations of new settlers, enough to make the American Republic an empire of liberty that had no need for entanglements or commitments to Europe.

Thus, Jefferson cast aside every roadblock that might have sat on the path to Western settlement. He cut the price of publicly owned lands in the West in order to make land purchase more affordable. He cut the minimum size required for the purchase in order to make such purchases more manageable for the individual farmer. He also turned a blind eye, for all practical purposes, to squatting on the public lands—in other words, that pioneers or farmers or entrepreneurs would simply—without buying the land from the federal government—set up shop on it, build a house, build a cabin, farm the ground, squat on it and, after a period of squatting, demand that their title to the ground, their title to that land be recognized. To that, Jefferson was happy to turn the blind eye. However those lands got settled, it was fine with him.

In some ways, Americans hardly needed much encouragement like that to move West, because the growth of the American population by natural increase and by immigration was already pushing people out of the older settled regions of the Atlantic coastline. In 1790, at the time of the first federal census, only about 100,000 white settlers lived in the western territories between the Appalachian Mountains and the Mississippi River. By 1800, the time of the second federal census, that number had already quadrupled to 400,000, twice as fast as the overall growth of the American population. After 1800, Jefferson's new land legislation and his new land policies turned this flow of immigration—which was already great—into a flood, spilling down the Ohio River from western Pennsylvania and over the western mountain passes of Virginia.

A chaotic and ungainly and unregulated sprawl of white squatters and settlers swept over a huge western triangle, that stretched from one point on Lake Erie, to a second point at Natchez on the Mississippi, and to a third point back to the Georgia coastline. By 1803, the state of Ohio was ready to be organized as a state, and was admitted as the 17th state in the union. By 1810, the entire trans-Appalachian white population had more than doubled again, to approximately one million. Ten years later, in 1820, it had doubled once more.

There was, however, one serious difficulty in the opening up of the trans-Appalachian territories. The further westward over the Appalachians the farmers moved, the more remote they became from the markets of the Atlantic coastline, and beyond them, of war-torn Europe, which was one of the chief markets for American exports of grain. That meant that the more costly and unprofitable it became to ship agricultural products back to New York or to Philadelphia, the harder the task for western farmers was going to be.

Now, western farmers could find a sort of temporary solution by simply abandoning any unreliable roads leading back eastward over the Appalachians, and they could send their grain in another direction, not eastwards to the Atlantic Coast, but south on cheaply built flatboats going down the river valleys of the Ohio, the Cumberland, and the Tennessee down to the Mississippi River and then, once on the Mississippi River, south to New Orleans, where the grain could then be sold and exported faster and at better prices than from New York or Philadelphia or Baltimore or Charleston.

The hitch to all of this was that New Orleans did not belong to the United States. It belonged at that time to Spain, and that meant that a foreign power held the chokepoint of Jefferson's new agricultural empire of liberty in the West. That hitch was compounded in 1800, when Napoleon Bonaparte bullied the feeble Spanish monarchy into signing over to his empire not only New Orleans, but the entire vast stretch of Spanish Louisiana.

Jefferson had turned westward to avoid entanglements in Europe, and now, in the shape of New Orleans, he suddenly faced the most serious European entanglement of them all. Napoleon Bonaparte, in fact, intended to do a good deal more than merely take possession of New Orleans. Bonaparte intended to resurrect the colonial empire in North America that France had lost to Britain at the end of the French and Indian War 40 years before. Napoleon had already taken the first step in the recreation of this French Empire by dispatching his brother-in-law, General Charles Victor Emmanuel Leclerc, and 20,000 veteran French troops to re-conquer the key Caribbean island of San Domingue, the island that today we refer to as Haiti and the Dominican Republic.

On San Domingue, the black slave population had taken advantage of the confusions of the French Revolution to overthrow their masters and declare independence as a native black republic. If

Napoleon succeeded in reestablishing himself on San Domingue and reestablishing French control of San Domingue, that would create a powerful French presence in the Gulf of Mexico and its immediate neighbor, the Mississippi River Valley. If that happened, then there was no limit to the mischief Bonaparte could cause the American Republic. The entire western agricultural traffic along the Mississippi and all of its tributaries west of the Appalachians could be held hostage in order to compel the cooperation of the United States with French foreign policy, or alternately, Napoleon could use promises of free trade to woo the settlers of the western territories to trade in their allegiance to the United States and join his new Louisiana empire.

To the surprise of two continents, however, General Leclerc and his French Army failed, in fact failed miserably in their attempt to re-conquer San Domingue for France. Since San Domingue was the key to the rebuilding of a French Empire in the New World, Napoleon's plans were knocked into a cocked hat and that, in turn, rendered Louisiana useless to Bonaparte.

In the spring of 1803, Napoleon decided to cut his losses. Thomas Jefferson had been vainly trying to protect American interests on the Mississippi by offering to buy the city of New Orleans and its district from the French. He had even sent a special emissary, James Monroe, to join the American Minister in Paris, Robert Livingston, in pressing an offer on the French. Through his Foreign Minister—the long-lived political survivor, Monsieur Talleyrand—Napoleon abruptly offered to sell not only New Orleans, but all of the Louisiana province to the Americans, approximately 830,000 square miles for $15 million in spot cash. Monroe and Livingston nearly choked with surprise and begged for time to consult with President Jefferson. Talleyrand demanded an immediate response, and so they agreed, signing a treaty on April 30, 1803, in what amounted to the single greatest real estate deal in history.

To the relief of Monroe and Livingston, Jefferson was delighted with the purchase, because the Louisiana Purchase more than doubled the amount of territory available for his agricultural empire of liberty. It also seemed to guarantee that the American Republic, for generations to come, would always have more than enough land to make every citizen a virtuous and independent farmer, and not one of those very strange bankers and manufacturers and merchants whom the Republicans deplored so greatly.

Now, to be sure, Jefferson was not a little troubled by the realization that the Constitution gave him no enumerated authority to purchase new land for the United States. Remember, that was the argument Jefferson had used against Hamilton and against the Bank of the United States a decade before. Well, Jefferson was quite well aware that the shoe was now on the other foot, and he even toyed with the idea of proposing an amendment to the Constitution that would grant the federal government the authority to acquire new land. Amending the Constitution was going to take time, however, and the French wanted a quick decision; thus, Jefferson sent the Treaty of Cession that ceded Louisiana to the United States, to the Senate with the private comment, "The less we say about constitutional difficulties, the better."

The Senate ratified the treaty in October, and American officials took formal possession of Louisiana in ceremonies at New Orleans on December 20. Two important details of the Louisiana Purchase, which had been overlooked in the hasty process of sale, were two things that you would suppose would be the most obvious things to be questioned about. Those were the boundaries of the Louisiana Territory and the contents of it. Talleyrand's descriptions of the boundaries of Louisiana were deliberately vague, because the French had not held title to Louisiana long enough to explore it all for themselves once the Spanish had been compelled to yield it up.

Consequently, it was not clear whether the purchase also included the Spanish held province of West Florida, that's the panhandle of the present day state of Florida, whether it included the vast plains down to the Rio Grande, the modern state of Texas, or the Oregon Territory on the Pacific, nor did anyone have a clear idea of what the geography, the inhabitants, or the resources of the new purchase looked like. Talk about buying things sight unseen. Jefferson himself had been pressing for some sort of expedition to the West to answer these questions ever since the days of the Confederation. The Livingston-Monroe negotiations merely gave him the pretext to ask Congress for the typically parsimonious sum of $2,500 to finance a scouting party up the Missouri River Valley to the Pacific in the spring of 1803.

Jefferson selected as chief for this expedition his reliable and enterprising private secretary, Captain Meriwether Lewis; Lewis chose as his associate William Clark. In the spring of 1804, shortly after the Treaty of Cession had been signed and the expedition relieved of the need to go up the Missouri Valley in secret, Lewis and Clark set off from St. Louis with a 48-man corps of discovery, and with instructions from Jefferson to thoroughly map the Louisiana Territory; evaluate its soil, its climate, and its mineral resources; and determine whether the Missouri River might not actually run all the way to the Pacific.

You see, not even Thomas Jefferson could escape one last attempt to discover that futile dream of the first European explorers of North America, a northwest passage to China. Lewis and Clark's expedition disappeared without a trace for two and a half years until, without any warning, they turned up back at St. Louis in September of 1806 with a loss of only one man on the journey. They had ascended the Missouri River as far as North Dakota. They had then wintered with the Mandan Indians, and they had scaled the Rocky Mountains with the help of a French Canadian trapper and his Shoshone Indian wife, Sacagawea. They had floated down the Snake and Columbia Rivers to the Pacific, and then returned over the Rockies in the summer of 1806.

The notebooks Louis and Clark brought back with them were packed with observations, sketches, and measurements; and the corps of discoveries pack train included specimens of plants and animals— also a family of Mandan Indians and even two grizzly bear cubs. They had had only one hostile skirmish with Indians, and they believed they had secured American title to the Oregon country as part of the purchase, simply by right of exploring it. It was the single greatest scientific expedition of the day.

In the end, it made only one major mistake in judgment: Both Lewis and Clark were agreed that the territory beyond the Missouri, while it was rich in natural resources, would never be fit for white settlement.

Lewis and Clark were only the first explorers to penetrate the vast spaces of the Louisiana Territory. In September of 1805, United States Army Lieutenant, Zebulon Pike, led another expedition up the Mississippi River to locate the sources of the Mississippi River. In 1806, Pike led a second expedition to explore the Rockies and Louisiana's uncertain boundary with the Spanish dominions in the

Southwest. He identified the Great Peak, which bears his name in modern Colorado, Pike's Peak, and managed to get himself arrested and briefly imprisoned by suspicious Spanish authorities in New Mexico.

The explorers were, in turn, followed by the entrepreneurs. A German-born fur dealer named John Jacob Astor set up a fur-trapping factory at the mouth of the Columbia River in 1810, and then laid the foundations for one of the greatest fortunes in American history. Over 600 freelance trappers—beginning with Jim Bridger, Jedadiah Smith, and Kit Carson—penetrated the Rockies by the 1830s in pursuit of valuable pelts and furs.

Following the entrepreneurs and trappers were the middlemen, who set up some 150 small posts and forts by the 1840s, to broker the fur trade in the Rockies. The strangest and the most sinister of these entrepreneurs was after far bigger game than beaver pelts, because he was no one less than Aaron Burr, Thomas Jefferson's first and not entirely welcome vice president.

Hardly any major figure in American political life has enjoyed so distinguished an ancestry as Aaron Burr. His father and namesake was an upstanding Presbyterian clergyman and an early president of Princeton. His mother, Esther, was a daughter of no one less than Jonathan Edwards. Unfortunately for the young Aaron Burr, death carried off both his father and his mother before he was four years old, and then killed off his famous grandfather shortly thereafter.

Over time, Burr was handed around the Edwards family to be cooed over, petted and, well, spoiled rotten. He grew to manhood oozing a lethal cloud of charm and ambition from the staggeringly handsome face and lustrous black eyes he inherited from the Edwards side of the family. He borrowed and he spent on a prodigal scale to gain access to New York politics and society, and he married a rich—but unlovely—widow in order to pay his debts. He allied himself politically with the Jeffersonians.

In 1800, Jefferson reluctantly accepted Burr as his vice presidential choice in order to secure New York's decisive electoral votes. Once elected, Jefferson promptly dropped Burr out of all his councils. In 1804, when Jefferson had enough momentum of his own to win easy reelection, he dropped Aaron Burr off the ticket entirely. Burr had become more than just the ordinary political liability to the

Republicans in 1804. As the most glamorous of the New York Republicans, Burr collided head on with Alexander Hamilton, who remained an influential voice in New York Federalism.

In July of 1804, Burr provoked Hamilton into a duel in which Burr, an expert pistol shot, mortally wounded Hamilton. To Burr's dismay, both Republicans and Federalists united in denouncing Burr as a murderer. Only a hasty flight out of state saved Burr from arrest. Hamilton's death ended all hope of Burr's career in politics, but that realization only kindled in Burr a darker hope of profiting by a career in treason. In the summer of 1804, while he was still actually serving as vice president, Burr secretly opened negotiations with the British Minister in Washington City, Anthony Merry.

Burr claimed that the western territories were seething with dissatisfaction at the United States government, and were willing to contemplate seceding from the American federal union to organize a separate republic in the Mississippi River Valley. With a little financial help from the British government, who, of course, would not be averse to seeing the American Republic divided, and with some guarantees of British protection, Burr could promise that at the right moment, he could rally the western settlers to his banner and proclaim a new Republic in the West.

Merry was cautiously skeptical, but, in fact, Burr had managed to recruit a ragtag band of followers. He borrowed money from his in-laws, and he flattered the commander of the American garrison in New Orleans, General James Wilkinson, into cooperation with his plot. The weak link in Burr's chain was General Wilkinson. On New Year's Day 1807, Burr assembled his tiny force at New Madrid on the Mississippi River.

He distributed arms and then announced his intention to capture Baton Rouge and make it his temporary headquarters. Burr did not realize it yet, but General Wilkinson in New Orleans had lost his courage at the last moment and betrayed Burr's scheme, so that at the very moment when Burr was preparing to hatch his plot, the local militia was on the way to arrest him and his cohorts. When he learned of Wilkinson's double-cross, Burr deserted his pathetic little army and stayed on the loose until February 19, when he was finally arrested by federal troops as he tried to escape into Spanish West Florida.

Burr was returned to Virginia, where he was put on trial for treason in the Federal District Court in Richmond, with the chief justice of the Supreme Court, John Marshall, presiding. The case against Burr turned out to be not clearly as self-evident as the government had hoped. Burr had cleverly covered the tracks of his intentions, and the government's witnesses against Burr, like General Wilkinson, were themselves suspicious and shady characters. Burr's attorneys, Edmund Randolph and John Wickham, quickly succeeded in turning the trial not into an evaluation of Burr's attempt at treason, but as a referendum on the administration of Thomas Jefferson. The chief justice, who of course had little love for Jefferson, beamed agreeably. On August 31, Marshall quashed the treason indictment of Burr on a technicality. Burr went off scot-free.

After several months of dodging his creditors, he smuggled himself in disguise on a boat for England. He returned from Europe in 1812, and when it became clear that his political friends in New York would make sure that he was not going to be arrested for the death of Alexander Hamilton, Burr boldly set up a law office on Nassau Street. He made only a scanty living, and he died in 1836. People pointed him out on the streets of New York City as the wickedest man alive.

The Burr conspiracy effectively demonstrated that the glories of the Louisiana acquisition were accompanied with some equally sizable risks. As the Burr trial splattered political sewage over Jefferson's reputation, though, and as the *Chesapeake* incident glaringly exposed the follies of disarming the military while international war was raging on the high seas, as New England Federalist governors publicly attacked the embargo, and as Chief Justice Marshall grinningly fenced in every move Jefferson made with one unassailable legal dictum after another, Jefferson's glorious "revolution of 1800" looked less and less like a mighty assertion of republican virtue and more and more like a confused mistake.

Depressed, overworked, and suffering from migraine, Jefferson would not even consider running for a third term as president in 1808. He wrote instead, "My longings for retirement are so strong that I, with difficulty, encounter the daily drudgeries of my duty." Well might the Republican cause have died with Jefferson's retirement had not the Republicans received a new lease on life from a highly unlikely quarter: the British.

Lecture Twenty
The Agrarian Republic

Scope:

All through his life, the one fixed and unmoving star in Thomas Jefferson's political philosophy was the importance of keeping the American Republic an overwhelmingly agrarian society. This agrarian culture was typified by independence, non-market agriculture, and community. No regard was paid to the claims of the North American Indians. As the much-feared Americans began pouring into Kentucky and the Northwest Territory in search of cheap land, the disheartened Indians chose one of two ways of dealing with this challenge: accommodation (as with the Seneca and Cherokees) or resistance (as in the revolt of Tenskwatawa and Tecumseh). On November 7, 1811, Tecumseh's brother Tenskwatawa unwisely led the Indians to attack an American army under William Henry Harrison, who defeated them and forced Tecumseh to seek refuge in Canada.

Outline

I. The fixed star in Jefferson's political philosophy was the need to keep America an agrarian society.

   A. Jefferson valorized farmers who owned their own land and lived off their own subsistence.

   1. This meant an antidevelopment posture.

   2. Nevertheless, it reflected much of the reality of early America.

   B. Jefferson was suspicious of the implications of market capitalism.

   1. Capitalism involved the exchange of goods at a profit and the conversion of those profits into more goods for exchange.

   2. It was perceived as a threat to the stability and ethical norms of many societies.

   3. No one did better in this than the English, who simplified the process through the conversion of economic exchange into cash.

   4. The English also set about overhauling their empire to balance supply and demand.

5. The American colonies were kept deliberately agricultural.
6. Jefferson inherited the system he loved from the people he hated.

II. Jefferson was also determined to keep America agrarian in culture.

   A. Agrarian culture was typified by independence.
      1. America had no aristocracy.
      2. Americans largely owned their land in fee simple.
      3. Wealth and power were diffused along a rough but recognizable equality.

   B. Agrarian culture was typified by non-market agriculture.
      1. Because land titles were not jeopardized by taxes, the chief incentive for production was household consumption.
      2. Farm households produced as much as 75 percent of what they required.
      3. Cash was almost nonexistent in many places as a medium of exchange.

   C. Agrarian culture was typified by patriarchy.
      1. The model for structuring the agrarian household was the rule of the adult male over women and children.
      2. Economic duties were divided along gender and age lines.
      3. Childhood scarcely existed as a separate category.

   D. Agrarian culture was typified by the influence of community.
      1. The absence of cash exchange demanded a face-to-face relationship.
      2. Indebtedness was common, without interest, and often not repaid.

III. The fatal flaw in this system was the increase in agricultural population.

   A. Reproduction of the subsistence household required the expansion of land to support it.
      1. This generated much of the westward expansion into the Northwest Territory.
      2. Such expansion spawned clashes with the Indian tribes of those regions.

B. Indian tribes were both numerous and well organized.
  1. Indian economies were fundamentally similar to Jefferson's.
  2. Instead of being a two-way relationship of colonists and British, the colonial economy was really three-way, including Indians.

C. As Americans poured into the Northwest Territory, Indians were confronted with two choices.
  1. They could accommodate themselves by signing over lands and accepting resettlement, by organizing themselves to mirror white society, or by undergoing revitalization.
  2. They could resist, a strategy adopted by Lalawethika, Tenskwatawa, and Tecumseh.

D. Resistance usually ended disastrously.
  1. Tecumseh's alliance was defeated at Tippecanoe in 1811.
  2. But it convinced Americans that the real enemy was the British.

Essential Reading:

Charles G. Sellers, *The Market Revolution*, chapter 1.

Supplementary Reading:

Christopher Clark, *The Roots of Rural Capitalism: Western Massachusetts, 1780–1861*.

Anthony F. C. Wallace, *The Death and Rebirth of the Seneca*.

Questions to Consider:

1. What would victory for the Tecumseh alliance have looked like if Tecumseh had been successful?
2. Does the agrarian ideal still have political force today?

Lecture Twenty—Transcript
The Agrarian Republic

All through his life the one fixed and unmoving star in Thomas Jefferson's political philosophy as a Republican was the importance of keeping the American Republic an overwhelmingly agrarian society. There was in Jefferson's mind an intimate and unbreakable link between political virtue and the independence enjoyed by the cultivator or husbandman. Jefferson wrote, "Those who labor in the earth are the chosen people of God, if ever he had a chosen people." Jefferson wrote in his notes on the state of Virginia, "It is in," he said, "in the breasts of the agriculturalists, that he has made his peculiar deposit for a substantial and genuine virtue. It is the focus in which he keeps alive that sacred fire which otherwise might escape from the face of the Earth, corruption of morals in the mass of cultivators is a phenomenon of which no age nor nation has furnished an example. The farmer who owned his own land and raised his own subsistence did not need to depend on the casualties and caprice of customers."

For that, Jefferson was critical to the development of a genuinely republican society, because dependence, including dependence on markets and dependence on customers, "begets subservience and venality, suffocates the germ of virtue and prepares fit tools for the designs of ambition."

Now, it was true that this might mean that America might never develop great merchant cities or great manufacturing centers, but "On the other hand," Jefferson thought, "the mobs of great cities add just so much to the support of pure government as sores do to the strength of the human body." Jefferson's praise of the mass of cultivators and his blasé willingness to bypass commercial wealth in favor of republican virtue sounds a little quaint, sounds a little unrealistic in modern ears, but in the 1790s the confidence with which Jefferson spouted those opinions about how wonderful farming and agriculture were, was rooted in a good deal of hard fact, rather than just mere private Republican fantasies.

Despite Alexander Hamilton's successes in founding a Bank of the United States, and sponsoring the development of American finance and manufacturing, the American population in 1800 really was a mass of cultivators; Jefferson did nothing to alter that fact while he was president.

In 1800, when England had only 36 percent of its population engaged in agriculture, the American Republic had anywhere between 75 percent to 90 percent of its population down on the farm. Even in the relatively more urbanized areas of the Delaware River Valley and New England, up to 70 percent of the people still were farmers. By contrast, America had only 33 towns with a population of more than 2,500, and only five of those—in this case Philadelphia, Baltimore, New York, Boston, and Charleston—held more than 20,000 people. Philadelphia, the largest city in the American Republic at 70,000 people hardly counted as a city in comparison to London with its one and a quarter million inhabitants.

Oddly, the people whom Jefferson had the most to thank for this situation were the British, or at least the former British colonial administrators of North America. This was because during the 1700s, Britain had emerged from a century of economic turmoil and political upheaval as one of the most successful examples of commercial capitalism in the world. Britain, you'll recall from our earlier lectures, was determined to treat its colonies in North America as suppliers for that success, not as rivals to it.

Which brings us at last to talking about capitalism. Capitalism, in the barest sense of the word, may be simply the most natural and spontaneous of all economic relationships, because in that barest sense capitalism means merely two things. One is the exchange of goods at a profit to oneself, and the second is the conversion of those profits into more goods for exchange, and thus more profits. No one did better in practice of commercial capitalism than the English. The English had the advantage of geographical position; they had favorable politics, and they had an impressive merchant marine that would carry the products of capitalism abroad and bring materials for its further support from far away.

Above all, the English greased the wheels of commercial capitalism by simplifying the very process of economic exchange, and they did that by converting most of their currency into easily portable paper money. Now, that paper money might take the form either of bills of exchange, which were issued between merchants, or as bank notes issued by the Bank of England.

The great thing about using cash, using paper money that way, was how impersonal it was. An economic transaction involving cash could be conducted at a distance, whereas a transaction involving farmed goods could not be carried on at a distance. If you're going to trade a cow, you've got to get that cow to some place else. That takes time and it's expensive, whereas if you're trading in paper money, well that's not a problem. It's light, it's portable, and it can be easily traded back and forth. Cash, for instance, always means the same thing, no matter who you're dealing with, whether it's a lifelong friend or a total stranger. Now, a cow is a different matter; friends and strangers can disagree about the value of a cow, but you sure can't disagree with that number marked on paper money.

Cash was also exact. It had that abstract numerical value that could be computed precisely and which would be computed apart from any sentimental or personal value. After all, people do not proffer a five-dollar bill or a 10-dollar bill, both paper money, and try to establish a value for it based upon sentiment, or kinship, or relation, or shared religion. Rather, that bill, if it's five dollars is always five dollars, or if it's 10 dollars it's always 10 dollars, and it doesn't matter who you are or how much you are loved or despised. It's still five dollars or 10 dollars—it's exact.

The success of the British in the development of commercial capitalism was only the beginning—for the sale of goods at a profit depends on two critical conditions. One is supply and the other is demand. There would be no goods to sell at a profit, whether for cash or for anything else, unless there was a guaranteed source of those goods, and at a price that a merchant could be sure would be attractive elsewhere.

Likewise there'd be no point in accumulating goods for sale unless there was a market for selling them; that required regulating the colonial economy in such a way that America produced goods for Britain, and that America provided a market for purchasing the goods from Britain. Nevertheless, America would never be permitted to develop any significant commercial mechanism for itself, because that would make America the rival of Britain. The result was that the American colonies were deliberately kept agricultural. Colonial merchants were severely restricted by taxes, by navigation acts, by the whole litany of legislation that we looked at in earlier lectures, and so America never came close during the colonial era to developing the grand commercial enterprises of their British counterparts; that was deliberate policy.

Now, this means that Thomas Jefferson, without wanting to admit it, had actually inherited the agrarian society he loved from the colonial administrators he hated, and what had once been a series of degraded and exploited agricultural colonies now suddenly turned into a perfectly formed agrarian Republic.

America, though, and this was what really delighted Jefferson, America had remained an agrarian Republic in more senses than just economics. The American Republic was not only dominated by an agrarian economy, it was dominated by an agrarian culture as well, because Jefferson's mass of cultivators also developed a peculiar social attitude along with their wheat, and rye, and barley.

This agrarian culture was typified by several things—first of all, by a passion for independence. Britain's North American colonies were not settled by aristocrats. That single fact had immense implications for the development of an agrarian society in America, since unlike Europe the absence of an aristocracy ensured that the American farmer had the opportunity to own land in his own name, instead of needing to rent or lease it from some nobleman who held prior title going back into the dim mists of the Middle Ages.

Moreover, there was enough cheap land available in America that each one of those farmers could expand his holdings virtually to whatever his powers of cultivation were, and that resulted in nearly every farmer having more or less the same size landholdings; most heads of farming households owned anywhere from 50 to 200 acres. In rural Hampshire County in western Massachusetts, 65 percent of the taxpayers owned their own land—owned it in fee simple, owned it clear. Ninety-two percent of all the houses were owned, not rented, not leased, but owned by the people living in them, and even the richest 10 percent of the county's farmers held only between 27 percent and 35 percent of the county's wealth on either side of 1800.

The agrarian society, the agrarian economy created a culture of independent landowners, where property and power were diffused along a rough and ready—but nevertheless recognizable—equality. The second thing that went into the making of an agrarian culture was its commitment to non-market agriculture, since land titles were not jeopardized by excessive taxes, fees, dues, or medieval obligations to great landlords. Since none of those were in place, the American farmers' chief incentive for producing things was for household or for local use. The further a farming region was located from markets the more likely it was to concentrate just its production on local consumption, since the cost of moving agricultural goods for sale easily grew prohibitive at more than two weeks' distance from markets.

Thus, taken as a whole, the American agricultural economy was primarily a subsistence surplus economy, in which farm households grew or produced as much as 75 percent of what they required, and then purchased the remaining 25 percent with a surplus of their own agricultural production. Farmers in Hampshire County who were sealed off from Boston by land distance, and from New Haven by falls and rapids on the Connecticut River, produced crops first and foremost for home consumption, and then used the surplus that was not consumed at home to barter for goods, liquor, tea, and dry goods, which a local shopkeeper or another farmer might produce. No more than 20 percent of the produce of the farm was sold off the farm in Hampshire County in 1820, and as late as 1870 not more than 40 percent of all American agricultural production was sold to outside markets.

Similarly, the more remote a farming district, the less likely it would be to rely on a single staple or cash crop, in which farmers would grow a single big money, big price staple crop exclusively, then sell that crop for cash, and then go out and buy everything they needed to live. Cash, in fact, was almost nonexistent in many places in the early Republic, and economic exchange in rural areas largely took the form of exactly what I described earlier, non-cash swapping of goods or produce, exchange of work, you know, a day helping with the barn raising in exchange for a day helping with harvest, and where there was some cash it got lent around in extended webs of indebtedness along networks dictated by kinship and by neighbors.

It was not impersonal, in fact it was very personal indeed, and the way in which the exchange was done, and the way in which what cash there was was lent about, was always done in terms of personal considerations and face-to-face arrangements. One other aspect of this agrarian culture was its passion for community.

The absence of cash exchange in rural districts not only created alternative forms of exchange, it demanded a particular model of community, in which non-cash exchange can take place. Without cash, economic exchange had to be personal; it had to be in the spirit of give and take, rather than buying and selling. It also required restraint, caution, and consideration of the other's ability to pay before repayment was demanded. In the agrarian culture debt was frequent—it was local, and it was unsystematic, and it was small, and often without any interest charged. Many farmers kept no account books at all; the account books that do survive show that three-fifths of all agricultural indebtedness was never repaid, and that the remaining two-fifths was repaid at times that varied from four months to thirteen and a half years. The idea of actually taking someone to court to collect such debts, well, that idea was looked upon as a violation of the spirit of neighborliness, and might be acted upon in that spirit.

The dominance of household production, local trade, the absence of a cash economy forced the inhabitants of a region into an integrated system of interdependence based on personal contact, rather than the abstract numerical use of cash. There was, however, one fatal flaw lurking in this idyllic agrarian scenario, and that was the problem caused by the rural farmers' production not of grain but of children.

On the average, the rural American family could expect the birth of eight to 10 children, and could expect to see eight or maybe six of them survive to become valuable parts of the household economy. Once those children reached adulthood themselves, though, they would be unable to perpetuate the pattern of rural subsistence and supply unless land was as easily available for them as it had been for their fathers. That, then, generated the great push westward, which filled up the old Northwest Territory and brought Kentucky, Tennessee, and Ohio into the Union, and which justified Jefferson's purchase of the Louisiana Territory.

The further these restless farmers penetrated into these territories, though, the more frequently they clashed with a race of people who already inhabited those territories, and who were not all that eager to surrender them. They, of course, were the North American Indians of the woodlands. It's a remarkable testimony to the racial tunnel vision of Western Europeans in the modern age that the original inhabitants of the North American continent were scarcely perceived as human beings, much less as having political, social, and economic systems as complex as the Europeans themselves. Thomas Jefferson lamented that "we have suffered so many of the Indian tribes already to extinguish," but he lamented that only on the grounds that this robbed him of specimens for his anthropological research on the origin of the human race. By his calculation, there were no more than about 30,000 Indians in North America.

Despite Jefferson's crocodile tears over their demise, the Indian tribes were, in fact, far from ready to be extinguished, and in fact they existed in a number of complicated social and economic relationships. The most basic unit of Indian political organization remained as it had been when white Europeans first landed in North America, and that was the tribe. Tribal identity was porous, though, and several tribes had created larger super tribes, federations, alliances, such as the Iroquois of the Northeast, and even individual tribes permitted the adoption of other Indians and even whites into tribal membership.

Nor were the numbers of Indians as few and as easily dismissed as Jefferson imagined; instead of 30,000 the Indian population of North America was probably closer to 750,000. What might have surprised Jefferson even more were the striking similarities that existed between Indian societies and the agrarian Republic he admired. Like rural Massachusetts farming communities, Indian tribes were generally patriarchal, with labor divided by gender and by age. In the case of the Shawnee, who were the largest tribal group in Kentucky and Ohio, adult males were responsible only for hunting, fishing, and the occasional war. Agriculture and child rearing fell entirely onto Indian women.

Even more like the whites, the Indians had learned—even before the Revolution—how to find places in the white man's commercial networks. Indians carefully managed and brokered the fur trade with white traders very much to their own economic advantage. We often think of the colonial economy as being a two-way exchange between colonists and European merchants, but it was much more a three-way arrangement, in which the Indians consciously played off colonists and British or French agents against each other.

All of this began to change with the French and Indian War, when the Indians placed most of their support behind the French and lost. Then, during the Revolution, the Indians mostly supported the British, hoping that a British victory would help to restrain aggressive colonial expansion over the Appalachian Mountains, but they lost again.

Now, as the much-feared Americans began pouring into Kentucky, and pouring into the Northwest Territory in search of cheap land, the disheartened Indian tribes chose one of two ways of dealing with this challenge. One was accommodation; accommodation usually meant the grudging but gradual sale or signing over of tribal lands to white settlement in return for various guarantees of protection or guarantees of resettlement further West. By the time of the Treaty of Fort Stanwix in 1784, the once-powerful Iroquois surrendered most of their lands in western New York and Pennsylvania. They had sided with the British during the Revolution, just as they had sided with the British during the French and Indian War, only in the Revolution they lost, and lost big.

In the Treaty of Hopewell in 1785, the Cherokees, who had also thrown in their lot with the British during the Revolution, gave up all of their claims on land in the Carolinas and Tennessee. In 1791, the part-white, part-Creek Indian chieftain Alexander McGilliveray reluctantly handed over all the Creek claims to land in Georgia. Sometimes accommodation meant the decision to internalize the white man's civilization and convert tribal ways into settled agricultural patterns, with the reasoning that if they did so then they could claim rights to the land in the same way that white people did. The Cherokees organized a common government for their villages, adopted a written legal code, and in 1827 devised a constitution, which among other things legalized black slavery and deprived any descendants of blacks from voting in tribal elections.

On the other hand, sometimes accommodation meant cycles of cultural collapse—the Seneca of western New York fell prey to alcoholism and poverty after the Revolution. They might have died out in time had not a middle-aged Seneca named Handsome Lake experienced a dramatic vision in 1799, which led to his creation of a new tribal religion. The Handsome Lake religion was a curious amalgam of Quakerism and traditional Seneca beliefs, but it revitalized the Senecas, and it eased them into patterns of moral behavior and land ownership that ensured the survival of the Seneca tribe.

The alternative to accommodation was resistance—for many other Indians' accommodation with the hated but victorious Americans was simply out of the question, and what was more their animosities were fed during the 1790s by British Canadians, who feared

American expansion just as much as the Indians, and who believed that the only way to restrain American expansion was the creation of an autonomous Indian buffer zone in the Northwest Territories.

Armed with British weapons and with their own indignation, the Indians of Ohio and Kentucky repeatedly tried to stop white expansion by force. The most dramatic example of this resistance began in 1805, when a Shawnee shaman named Lalawethika, the Prophet, experienced a vision not unlike that of Handsome Lake, and emerged from his vision with a new name, Tenskwatawa, the Open Door, and a new creed for the Shawnee, which rejected assimilation to white culture.

By 1809, Tenskwatawa's brother, Tecumseh, began joining his brother's religious vision of plans for a general Indian confederation and joint armed resistance to the whites. "Tecumseh," as William Henry Harrison, the territorial governor for the Indiana Territory once described him, "was one of those uncommon geniuses which spring up occasionally to produce revolutions and overturn the order of things."

Well, he certainly overcame the customary unwillingness of Indian tribes to cooperate with each other, and by 1811 Tecumseh had got as far as uniting the Wyandot, Chippewa, Sauk and Foxes, Winnebago, and Potawatomi tribes behind him. At the same time, though, Governor Harrison decided to take no chances and organized a force of militia to attack Tecumseh's capital, Prophet's Town on the Tippecanoe River, while Tecumseh was away negotiating with the Creeks and the Cherokees. Tecumseh's brother Tenskwatawa unwisely led the Indians out on November 7, 1811, to attack Harrison, who defeated them, humbled Tenskwatawa, and burned Prophet's Town to the ground. Tecumseh's alliance fell apart, and Tecumseh himself was forced to seek refuge with the British in Canada.

Tecumseh's flight to Canada became a symbol of a deadly cycle of suspicion and expansion; the agrarian society so beloved of Thomas Jefferson existed to provide a virtuous alternative to the corruption of Britain's international network of commercial capitalism. However, that society could not survive without constant expansion westward, which brought Americans into serious and often fatal confrontation with the Indian tribes. These tribes were both armed and encouraged by the British in Canada, who believed they had as much to fear as the Indians from American expansion.

This brought the cycle of suspicion back to the beginning, as Americans now concluded that the root of their difficulty in perpetuating a virtuous republican society in the West was once again—as it had been before in the 1760s—the British. The short-term solution was to do as William Henry Harrison did, and strike down the Indians before they struck; the long-term solution was to strike instead at the dark force that every Jeffersonian Republican had always been certain was plotting the destruction of the virtuous Republic, and that dark force was Great Britain.

Lecture Twenty-One
The Disastrous War of 1812

Scope:

Jefferson carefully hand-picked his own secretary of state, James Madison, as his successor; nonetheless, the congressional elections of 1808 and 1810 added to Congress not only a number of stubborn Federalists, but also wild-eyed young Republicans from the West who were convinced that the Republican leadership had not gone nearly far enough in dealing with the British. These *War Hawks* had no hesitation in predicting that the Americans could easily bring the British to heel by invading Canada, holding it hostage to good British behavior on the oceans, and, perhaps, even adding it to America's republican empire. In 1812, Madison sent a request to Congress for a declaration of war. The actual course of the war, which became known as the *War of 1812*, was a disaster. The only consistent successes the American army enjoyed were in the South, in Georgia and the Mississippi Territory, and in Andrew Jackson's successful defense of New Orleans. In October 1814, the Massachusetts legislature passed a peace resolution and organized a convention at Hartford, Connecticut, threatening secession from the Union. Only the signing of the Treaty of Ghent at the end of 1814 ended talk of a New England separatist movement.

Outline

I. American commerce had frequently been caught in the crossfire of the Napoleonic Wars.

    A. The British reserved the right to board American ships looking for "deserters."

        1. This triggered such incidents as the *Caravan* and the *Diana*, and the *Diana* and the *Topaz*.

        2. Jefferson attempted to deal with this by imposing an embargo on American high-seas commerce.

    B. The embargo failed to ease these confrontations.

        1. It wrecked the American economy.

        2. It wrecked the Republicans' hold on the government; they retained the presidency by electing James Madison but lost other political ground to the Federalists.

C. The surviving Republicans in Congress were Jeffersonian radicals from the West who demanded retaliation against the British.

    1. Henry Clay of Kentucky vigorously attacked the British abroad and corporate privilege at home.

    2. He was joined by the *War Hawks*.

    3. They demanded the seizure of Canada as a hostage to British behavior toward American shipping on the oceans.

D. President Madison preferred diplomatic dealings, but the British undid all his efforts.

    1. British correspondence with New England Federalists revealed a plot to detach New England from the United States.

    2. In April 1812, Madison finally asked a willing Congress for a declaration of war against Britain.

II. The United States was woefully unprepared to wage war, much less against the British.

A. Jefferson's administration had severely underfunded the American military.

    1. The federal budget was incapable of supporting a war.

    2. The U.S. Army listed only 7,500 men.

    3. The U.S. Navy had only 16 ships in commission.

B. The military results of the war were humiliating for the United States.

    1. General William Hull surrendered Detroit.

    2. General Stephen Van Renssalaer invaded Canada but was forced to retreat.

    3. General W. H. Harrison's expedition to recover Detroit was massacred at the Raisin River.

    4. General James Wilkinson's army invaded upper Canada but went wild and burned the town of York.

C. Actual American victories were few and insubstantial.

    1. Oliver H. Perry defeated the British Navy's Lake Erie squadron and forced the evacuation of Detroit.

    2. General W. H. Harrison won a subsequent victory at the battle of Thames, where Tecumseh was killed.

3. General Jacob Brown invaded Canada and defeated the British at Chippewa and Lundy's Lane but had to withdraw.
   D. The British launched their own counterinvasions in 1814.
      1. Admiral George Cockburn raided the American coast and burnt Washington.
      2. Sir George Prevost invaded New York but was stopped at Plattsburgh by Alexander Macomb and Thomas MacDonough.

III. The most substantial American successes were at sea and in the South.
   A. The American frigates failed to loosen a British blockade but scored several spectacular ship-to-ship battles.
      1. The *Constitution* fought and defeated the *Guerriere* and the *Java* (1812).
      2. The *United States* defeated the *Macedonian*.
      3. The *Essex* raided British shipping in the Pacific.
   B. "Red Stick" Creeks were roused by Tecumseh to attack American settlements.
      1. The Tennessee militia under Andrew Jackson crushed the Red Sticks at Horseshoe Bend (1814).
      2. Jackson occupied Spanish West Florida.
      3. Jackson then repulsed a British attack on New Orleans.

IV. By 1815, both Americans and British were ready for peace.
   A. The American war effort was exhausted.
      1. The treasury was depleted, and the war was being financed by borrowing.
      2. American commerce was suffering from the blockade.
   B. The British were also exhausted.
      1. The defeat of Napoleon at Leipzig in 1813 allowed the British to hope for all-around peace.
      2. The British offered to begin direct negotiations at Ghent.
   C. New England Federalists organized a break-away convention at Hartford.
      1. New England had suffered more than any other region.
      2. The Hartford Convention demanded new constitutional amendments to limit Madison's powers and threatened a

second convention for the purpose of seceding from the Union.

3. The signing of the Peace of Ghent ended these plans, but the effects of the War of 1812 would be felt for the next 40 years.

Essential Reading:

Donald Hickey, *The War of 1812*.

Supplementary Reading:

James M. Banner, *To the Hartford Convention*.

Robert Vincent Remini, *The Battle of New Orleans*.

Questions to Consider:

1. What would have been the consequences had Jackson failed to prevent a British seizure of New Orleans?

2. In what ways was the War of 1812 a direct result of Jefferson's policies?

Lecture Twenty-One—Transcript
The Disastrous War of 1812

In July of 1807, an American merchant ship, the brig *Caravan*, out of Boston, sailed into the harbor of Macaw, an island off the southern coast of China, where the Portuguese did a lively trade as middlemen between American shippers and the Chinese mainland. A British warship, the brig *Diana*, hove to beside the *Caravan* and demanded permission to board the American ship in order to take off an alleged "deserter" from the British Navy who was supposed to be hiding among the *Caravan*'s crew.

Captain Gilcrist of the *Caravan* wrangled with the lieutenant commanding the British vessel and, losing both time and patience, the British officer forced his way onto the deck of the *Caravan* with 30 or 40 men armed with cutlasses and pistols. When the British singled out several crew members at random as British deserters, Captain Gilcrist went wild, but wild or not, the British had the advantage of numbers and weapons.

They knocked Gilcrist down, tied him up, tied up his first officer, and seized his second officer as a guarantee of good behavior from the Americans. Then, on August 7, another American merchant ship—the Baltimore schooner *Topaz*—sailed into Macaw, and she too was stopped by the *Diana*. Captain Nichols of the *Topaz* was even more cantankerous than the master of the *Caravan*, and when a boat from the *Diana* came alongside the *Topaz* in order to board the American ship, Captain Nichols presented a blunderbuss and shot and wounded the lieutenant of the *Diana*. The British then swarmed up over the side of the schooner, shot down Captain Nichols, who expired immediately, and took possession of the *Topaz* and her cargo, charging her with piracy.

Now these incidents at Macaw might have attracted a lot more publicity and a lot more outrage than they did if they had not occurred in the shadow of the *Chesapeake* and *Leopard* incident that June, but they did, nevertheless, reinforce the sense of helplessness that American ship owners and merchants felt at being caught on the high seas between the warring navies of Napoleon's France and Great Britain. President Jefferson's answer to these outrages was, you'll remember, the embargo, but the embargo hurt the American economy far faster than it did the French or the British, and by the time Jefferson left office in March of 1809, the embargo was as good as dead.

In fact, the embargo not only wrecked American commerce, it had nearly wrecked the Republican Party's hold on the presidency. In 1808, at the end of his increasingly unhappy second term as president, Jefferson carefully hand-picked his own secretary of state, James Madison, as his successor and had him endorsed by the Republican caucus in Congress as the official Republican nominee, but the Federalists ran a sprightly anti-embargo campaign behind Charles Cotesworth Pinckney.

Even though Madison won the election of 1808, Pinckney swept all of New England, and Federalist congressional nominees picked up 24 seats in Congress. That still left a Republican majority, but the Republican majority that survived in Congress turned out to be almost as bad for James Madison's peace of mind as the new Federalist contingent. The congressional elections of 1808 and 1810 not only added to Congress a number of stubborn and uncooperative Federalists who believed that the Republicans had gone too far in provoking Britain, but they also added wild-eyed young Republicans from the new frontier western districts who were convinced that the Republican leadership had not gone nearly far enough in dealing with the British.

Henry Clay, who had been elected as Kentucky's junior senator in 1806, placed the blame for America's repeated humiliations at sea— like those of the *Topaz*, the *Caravan*, and the *Chesapeake*—squarely on the shoulders of the hated British. "I scarcely know of an injury that France could do us, short of an actual invasion of our territory, that would induce me to go to war with her," Clay declared, "whilst the injuries we have received from Great Britain remain un-redressed."

Now Clay's agitation was fueled by more than just simple rage over the high-handedness of several British Navy officers. Clay was born in Virginia in 1777, made a successful career as a lawyer in Kentucky, and came to Congress as a thorough-going Republican, a card-carrying enemy of banks, corporations, and aristocratic privilege.

When Hamilton's old Bank of the United States came up for re-chartering by Congress in 1811, Clay helped to sink it for good.

"What was the use of the bank?" Clay demanded in good Republican fashion. Clay said, "It is a splendid association of favored individuals taken from the mass of society and invested with exemptions and surrounded by immunities and privileges." Down went the bank.

Similarly, as a westerner, Clay viewed the Indian disturbances on the frontier through Republican eyes. In other words, it was a British plot to slow—or maybe even contain permanently—the growth of the American republic. Therefore, Indian trouble on the frontier, harassment of American ships on the high seas, it was all of a piece—all one great British plot—to undo the American Revolution.

Clay was not alone in thinking this way. He was joined in Congress by a cadre of western Republicans like himself who were dubbed the *War Hawks*, and they were called that because none of them had any hesitation in predicting that the American army and the militia of the American states could easily bring the British to heel by invading Canada, and once having invaded Canada, hold it hostage to good British behavior on the oceans and, who knows, maybe in time even add Canada to America's republican empire.

President Madison, on the other hand, preferred diplomacy and restraint as the solutions to the challenges, either imagined or real, that the British had offered to the United States, but in the spring of 1812, Madison's secretary of state—James Monroe—quietly obtained copies of correspondence belonging to one John Henry, an Irish-born New Yorker who had acted as the secret agent of Sir James Craig—the British governor of upper Canada. Entirely on his own cracked-brained initiative, Craig hired Henry in 1809 to open contact with any New England Federalists who might be willing to quit the Republican-dominated American Union and attach New England to Canada. Henry didn't get very many takers for his plot and, what was more, he got very little thanks for his efforts from the British.

Consequently, Henry turned and sold copies of his correspondence with New Englanders, with the British, he sold them all to Monroe for $50,000, which was a lot of money in 1812. On March 9, 1912, President Madison forwarded copies of this correspondence to Congress.

Now, the Henry papers and the Henry-Craig plot were obviously a serious embarrassment to Federalists in Congress but, even more, they moved the *War Hawks* to push President Madison right to the brink with the British. With American ships being pillaged at sea, and with British subversion working alternately to seduce New England and to seduce the western Indians, "The next step," as Secretary of State Monroe announced in April of 1812, "is war."

In mid-May, the Republican congressional caucus met to select the Republican presidential nominee for the elections in the fall of 1812 and, led by Henry Clay, the caucus plainly told James Madison that his being supported as the party candidate for the next presidency depended upon his screwing his courage to a declaration of war. Thus, on June 1, Madison sent a request to Congress for a declaration of war. The Federalists in the Senate slowed the measure down, but they could not stop it, and a war bill passed the Senate on June 17. The next day, Madison signed it.

On the surface, no country was more ill-prepared to wage war in 1812 than the United States, much less to wage it against Great Britain. Twelve years of Republican rule had successfully whittled the national budget and national taxes to one-fifteenth the size of Britain's. The American army had only 7,500 men on its rolls, and they were commanded either by inexperienced junior officers or by senile veterans of the American Revolution. The American Navy, thanks to Jefferson's parsimony, consisted of exactly 16 commissioned warships, seven frigates, and an assortment of sloops and gunboats, as compared to the 116 frigates and 124 mammoth ships of the line of the British Navy, but the Americans were remarkably untroubled by these odds.

It was confidently expected that the bulk of the British Army and the bulk of the British Navy would be pinned down by their war against Napoleon in Europe, while Canada would be able to offer only the resistance of the 5,600 poorly organized British regulars who made up the entire Canadian garrison force. Canada was ripe for the picking. The actual course of the war, which became known by the rather lackluster title of the *War of 1812*, as though they couldn't quite figure out what else to call it, turned out to be immensely more humiliating than Madison or any of the *War Hawks* had expected.

Madison's secretary of war, William Eustis, had drawn up a war plan that provided for a three-pronged invasion of Canada. Talk about optimism. The westernmost prong, with 2,000 regular American infantry under the aging and ailing General William Hull, would jump off from Fort Detroit and occupy the southern tip of upper Canada. Hull would then be joined by the central prong of 2,600 regulars and 3,500 New York state militia under Stephen Van Renssalaer, and they would cross over the Niagara River, link forces with Hull, and complete the conquest of upper Canada, and then there was the easternmost prong of the attack under General Henry Dearborn, which would move out from Plattsburgh, New York, and up Lake Champlain towards Montreal and lower Canada.

Nearly nothing went right with any of this. Hull spent most of the summer of 1812 just getting from Dayton, Ohio, to Fort Detroit, and when Hull crossed over into lower Canada, he quickly lost his nerve and fell back to Detroit, where a small force of British regulars, Canadian militia, and about 1,000 Indians forced him to surrender without firing a shot. Stephen Van Renssalaer successfully crossed the Niagara River on October 16, 1812, and overran a British force on the Queenstown Heights overlooking the river, but Renssalaer found more trouble behind him than in front of him. Renssalaer's rank as general in command was based on his commission as an officer in the New York state militia.

The senior officer of the United States regulars contingent in this force—Brigadier General Alexander Smythe—announced that he would not take orders from a militia officer, and withheld his regulars from cooperating with Renssalaer. As British reinforcements came up, Renssalaer had no choice but to retreat back across the Niagara. Smythe tried to launch his own invasion across the Niagara in November, but this time the New York state militia refused to take orders from him, and went home.

Dearborn changed his own plans and, instead of moving on Montreal, moved west along the St. Lawrence river, all the while trying unsuccessfully to persuade his militia that it was not a violation of their constitutional rights as state militia to order them onto Canadian soil.

Well, the blunders of the year 1812 were bad enough, but the affairs of the year 1813 promptly went from bad to worse. William Henry Harrison, the hero of Tippecanoe, was put in charge of American operations in the western territories, and told to repair the damage done by Hull's shameful surrender at Fort Detroit; however, the first force Harrison sent to recover Fort Detroit was stopped by a mixed

British-Canadian-Indian force on the Raisin River on January 22 and massacred afterward by the Indians.

The blundering Brigadier General James Wilkinson, the same James Wilkinson who double-crossed Aaron Burr in 1804, crossed Lake Ontario in April of 1813 and even captured the town of York, but his men went on a rampage afterwards, looting and burning the town to the ground. Almost the only satisfaction the Americans could take for their troubles was purchased not by the army easily walking over Canada, but by the navy.

Naval Lieutenant Oliver Hazard Perry, who was sent to command the tiny naval base at Presque Isle on Lake Erie, bought or built from scratch a 12-ship flotilla of gunboats and small armed vessels, and in September of 1813, he led them out in search of the British Lake Erie squadron. Remarkably, he found them, and in an all-day battle on September 10, sank or captured the entire British squadron. In one stroke, Perry accomplished what the army had failed to do in two years. By controlling Lake Erie, Perry made upper Canada militarily indefensible by the British.

The British evacuated Fort Detroit and abandoned most of upper Canada to William Henry Harrison. Among the retreating British was Harrison's old nemesis, Tecumseh, who persuaded the British to make one last stand on the Thames River. Reluctantly, the British agreed, but Harrison's Kentucky militia broke the British lines and scattered them. Tecumseh, trying to rally his Indian followers, was shot down, and Kentucky militiamen cut strips of flesh from his legs to use as razor straps. Unfortunately for the American army, they found no way to exploit the gains they had made by the end of 1813.

When the next campaign season opened in the spring of 1814, a well-organized American force under a fighting Quaker—there's a contradiction in terms—named Jacob Brown crossed the Niagara River yet again and soundly defeated the British at Chippewa on July 8, and then fought the British to a bloody draw at Lundy's Lane on July 25; Brown's losses from both battles were too great to permit him to continue the invasion, however. Instead, it was the turn of the British to launch their own major counter-invasions.

The first—composed of 11,000 troops newly released from the European wars—would step off from Montreal and move south on New York City. The second—a combined army-navy operation under Admiral George Cockburn—would raid the American coast, and the third part of this plan under Major General Edward Pakenham, would capture New Orleans and thus throttle the American West. Coburn's combined fleet operation struck first.

The British sailed boldly and bare-facedly into the Chesapeake Bay with hardly any opposition in June of 1814, landing virtually at will to burn several towns, and in August of 1814, pushing inland to burn the capital, Washington City, itself. Only the stubborn defense put up by the garrison of Fort McHenry in Baltimore Harbor during the night of September 13 through 14, 1814, prevented the British from putting Baltimore to the torch as well.

The Fort McHenry garrison's resistance so impressed one onlooker, a Baltimore lawyer named Francis Scott Key, that the next morning he wrote a poem in honor of the event by the name of "The Star-Spangled Banner." The particular flag he was talking about was a gigantic garrison version of this 15-star and, notice, 15-stripe flag, and a large garrison version of this still flies today at Fort McHenry in Baltimore Harbor.

Congress had not yet quite figured out that while you have room to multiply the number of stars, the more states you add, if you also add stripes, will make for a very big and bulky flag. After this flag, Congress wisely decreed that the stripes would be limited to 13 in honor of the original 13 colonies, the original 13 states, and the number of stars in the union of the flag would be what really indicated the number of states in the Union, but this at least, 15 stars and 15 stripes, was what Francis Scott Key that night so proudly hailed in the twilight's last gleaming as Fort McHenry resisted the British invaders, and successfully.

The British land invasion from Canada fared somewhat less well than Cockburn's raiding of the American coast. Sir George Prevost, with those British troops, veterans of the Napoleonic Wars, newly arrived in Canada, cut a wide swath south into New York along Lake Champlain, but at Plattsburgh, a joint defensive action by Brigadier General Alexander Macomb and Commodore Thomas MacDonough's little fleet on Lake Champlain, stopped Prevost and the British in their tracks and forced them to retreat back to Canada.

The prominence of little fleets like Thomas MacDonough's and Oliver Hazard Perry's, points up the most surprising aspect of the

War of 1812 for the Americans, and that was the success of the U.S. Navy. No one had seriously expected the U.S. Navy to take on the British Navy in a major fleet action and, in truth, the handful of American frigates did nothing or next to nothing to prevent the British Navy from clamping a severe blockade on American seaports but, let loose on their own on the oceans, the American frigates scored some spectacular one-on-one victories against the greatest naval power on earth. The frigate *Constitution* met and captured the notorious British frigate *Guerriere* in a single combat off Halifax in August of 1812, and then sank the British frigate *Java* in December of 1812.

The frigate *United States* captured the British frigate *Macedonian* in October 1812, and the sloop *Hornet* captured the British sloop *Peacock* the next year. The smaller frigate, *Essex*, captured the British sloop *Alert* and then proceeded to the South Pacific, where the *Essex* picked off 15 British merchant men before a British squadron finally cornered her off the coast of Chile and pounded her to pieces in 1814.

By contrast, the only consistent successes the U.S. Army enjoyed were in the South in Georgia and the Mississippi Territory, where Tecumseh, before his death at the Battle of the Thames, had successfully roused the radical young bloods of the Creek Indians to war against the Americans. About 2,000 "Red Stick" Creeks, they were called that because of the red sticks Tecumseh had given them as a signal for an uprising, raided American forts and American settlements along the Alabama River, and in August of 1813, they massacred almost every white defender of Fort Mims near the border with Spanish West Florida.

The War Department could spare few regulars to deal with the Creeks, but the secretary of war did authorize the major general of the Tennessee militia—a rawboned judge and former congressman named Andrew Jackson—to summon volunteers to deal with the Red Sticks. Well, Jackson did more than deal with the Red Sticks. With 2,000 militiamen behind him, he crushed the Red Sticks at the Battle of Horseshoe Bend in March of 1814, and then forced them to sign a treaty yielding 22 million acres of their lands in the Mississippi Territory to the United States. Then, without hesitating, he set off in pursuit of renegade Red Sticks, crossing over the border with Spanish Florida in November of 1814 and occupying Pensacola, which he then claimed for the United States—totally without justification from the Department of State, but that was beginning to set a pattern for Andrew Jackson.

Then, when word reached him of the planned British assault on New Orleans, Jackson doubled back up the coast, fortified the approaches to New Orleans and, on January 8, 1815, threw back a major British assault after suffering only 13 casualties, as opposed to over 2,000 British dead, cut down in heaps by the deadly rifle fire of Jackson's loyal Kentucky and Tennessee militiamen.

As it turned out, the British might have saved themselves the trouble of the New Orleans debacle. As President Madison advised Congress in 1813, the few victories the Americans had won had depleted the treasury to the bottom. The republic was functioning on borrowed money, recruiting was at a standstill, and the British blockade was choking American commerce to death. What was worse: The European wars had come to an end that fall with the collapse of Napoleon at the Battle of Leipzig and that, of course, left the British free to turn their veteran armies loose on the American republic at just the point when the Americans were growing weary of the struggle.

In the summer of 1813, the emperor of Russia offered to mediate between the British and the Americans, but the proposal was rejected by the British. Six months later, the British, who were suffering more than Madison realized from their own war weariness, offered to open direct negotiations for peace. Madison responded at once. He sent three commissioners, including the *War Hawk* Henry Clay, to the Belgian city of Ghent to dicker for peace terms.

In New England, however, the Federalists did not wait to have Madison tell them that the war was going badly, or that it was time to make peace. They knew it themselves. No region had suffered more from the British blockage than New England, and no region had less reason to trust Madison's Republican agents in Ghent. In October of 1814, the Massachusetts legislature, top-heavy with disgruntled Federalists, passed a peace resolution and urged the New England states to make arrangements for a separate peace treaty with Britain. Sneering at the war as "Mr. Madison's war," the New Englanders went so far as to organize a convention in Hartford, Connecticut, in December of 1814, with 22 delegates from all the New England states demanding new constitutional amendments to corral

Madison's powers, threatening to call a second convention in Boston for the purpose of seceding from the Union if their demands were not met.

In the end, it never came to that. The messengers the Hartford Convention sent to Washington City to deliver the convention's ultimatums arrived in the fire-blackened capital to find the city celebrating Jackson's victory at New Orleans and, more to the point, celebrating the signing of the peace treaty at Ghent. The War of 1812 was over, but its after-effects would be felt for the next 40 years.

Lecture Twenty-Two
The "American System"

Scope:

The War of 1812 collapsed the U.S. Treasury, bankrupted hundreds of businesses, and soaked up the tiny hoard of American financial capital by government borrowing. Madison proposed a series of initiatives—a new military, a second Bank of the United States, and a national transportation network. Henry Clay and John C. Calhoun became the principal spokesmen for what came to be called *National Republicanism.* Clay's proposals for rebuilding the infrastructure of the American economy after 15 years of Jeffersonianism became known as the *American System.* The key to understanding the depth of the appeal of the National Republicans lies in the invention of the cotton gin, the opening of the Mississippi valley to cotton agriculture, the development of steam-powered transportation, canal building (as in the Erie Canal), and finally, the steam-powered railroad. But the greater the distance involved in selling agricultural goods, the more farmers were forced to turn to borrowing on distant credit markets and to the impersonal and abstract form of cash exchange.

Outline

I. The War of 1812 forced the Republican leadership into a series of initiatives that threatened a serious departure from Jeffersonian orthodoxy.

   A. President Madison called for reviving the American military.
   1. New fortifications, an enlarged army, and a naval construction program were proposed.
   2. To fund this, Madison asked for a continuance of wartime taxes and a doubling of the tariff rates.

   B. Madison also called for a revival of the Bank of the United States.
   1. A second bank would be chartered along lines similar to Hamilton's.
   2. It would be capitalized at $35 million.

C. Madison also proposed a national transportation initiative.

    1. He found his principal floor leaders in Congress in sadder-but-wiser War Hawks, such as Clay and Calhoun.

    2. These initiatives became known as *National Republicanism*.

D. These departures shocked Republican elders.

    1. Jefferson predicted that they would concentrate power and money in their own hands.

    2. Republicans sought an uncontroversial presidential candidate for 1816 in James Monroe.

II. President Monroe disappointed old-guard Republicans by continuing Madison's policies.

A. None of this would have been practicable without a workable system of national transportation.

    1. The Cumberland Road project was hesitatingly supported by Madison and Monroe and followed by state turnpike projects.

    2. Steam-powered riverboats, beginning with Robert Fulton's *Clermont*, further cut shipping costs, especially on the Mississippi River.

    3. Canals provided artificial waterways to supplement the rivers, the most spectacularly successful being DeWitt Clinton's Erie Canal (1825).

    4. Railroads, introduced from Britain in 1828, cut shipping costs still further.

B. The result was the undercutting of the agrarian economy and culture.

    1. Households stopped producing their own support and turned commercial.

    2. Face-to-face reciprocity yielded to formal contract and distant market obligations.

    3. Following the second Bank of the United States, new banks sprang into life with state charters, issuing a flood of paper bank notes.

C. Monroe's two terms as president became known as the *era of good feelings*.

    1. Anxieties diminished as the social costs of market capitalism were outweighed by the prosperity that resulted.

2. Nevertheless, Jefferson looked at the postwar policies as a betrayal of republicanism.

Essential Reading:

Harry L. Watson, *Liberty and Power*.

Supplementary Reading:

Robert Dawidoff, *The Education of John Randolph*.

Carol Sheriff, *The Artificial River*.

Questions to Consider:

1. Why were Jeffersonians so suspicious of banks?
2. To what degree were slavery and Indian removal the byproducts of economic decisions?

Lecture Twenty-Two—Transcript
The "American System"

The War of 1812 started badly and, except for Andrew Jackson's lame duck victory at New Orleans two weeks after the signing of the Treaty of Ghent, it ended badly, too. Henry Clay—who as one of the team of treaty negotiators—was part and parcel of the negotiations at Ghent. Clay admitted that, after signing the treaty, the terms turned out to be different from what was expected when the war was made. Oh, indeed they were, because the war taught many of the Republicans some unpleasant lessons about the workability of many of the ideas that Mr. Jefferson's "revolution of 1800" had been built upon.

I mean, think about it. Republicans were supposed to hate banks, but if the Bank of the United States had not been allowed to expire in 1811, the secretary of the treasury could have borrowed the 18 million dollars he needed to finance the war from the Bank of the United States; since there was no Bank of the United States left—its charter having expired and no renewal having been adopted—without that bank the secretary of the treasury was forced to cut an unappealing deal with John Jacob Astor of New York and Stephen Girard of Philadelphia for personal loans to keep the country afloat.

In addition, Republicans, remember, were supposed to keep the independent farmer free from the fatal drag of taxation, but a government that does not tax cannot pay for national roads or other internal improvements, or for an army or navy, and the pitiful small showing of the American frigates on the seas, as well as the haphazard performance of the American army having to cut its own roads through the forests just to get to the Canadian border, all of that underscored the folly of small-scale government.

James Madison was not the first Republican to realize these things, but he was the most important, and so in 1816, his last year in office, Madison proposed to the 14th Congress a series of new initiatives that soon had the retired and white-haired Thomas Jefferson wondering who it was he had passed the presidency to.

These initiatives fall mainly into three categories. With America's military follies still fresh in everyone's mind, Madison asked for a new system of coastal fortifications, an enlarged army, and a naval construction program that pledged a million dollars annually for 10 years in order to build nine ships of the line and nine new frigates. To pay for these programs, Madison asked Congress for a continuance of three million dollars in wartime property taxes, and doubling of the current tariff rates so that foreign imports would be taxed at a rate of 20 percent across the boards and 25 percent for imported textiles.

Madison next presented Congress with a scheme for reviving the Bank of the United States, and he proposed a re-chartering of the bank along lines identical to that originally proposed by Hamilton, except that now Madison wanted to triple the second bank's capitalization to 35 million dollars.

The last piece of the new postwar agenda was introduced in December of 1816, and provided for the construction of a national road system, to be funded by revenue that the second Bank of the United States would generate for the government in bank stock dividends.

Now, Madison's enthusiasm alone could not have carried these measures over the horrified opposition of old-line Virginia Republicans in Congress like John Randolph and John Taylor. On the other hand, Madison was not the only Republican who had been shocked silly by the War of 1812, and who was willing to trim a little off Republican purity in order to guarantee national security. Madison found floor leaders in Congress in two of the most arch young Republican War Hawks, Henry Clay and John C. Calhoun. As if to atone for pushing the nation into a war that their own Republican ideology had left utterly unprepared to wage, Clay and Calhoun became the principal spokesmen for what came to be called *National Republicanism*. Clay announced his conversion to National Republicanism in a major speech to Congress on January 16, 1816, and went on to endorse the new military program, what he called "a chain of turnpikes, roads, and canals from Passamaquoddy to New Orleans and, in addition to those, tariffs to effectually protect our manufacturers."

Then, there was Calhoun; Calhoun argued, "National greatness is the best guarantee of liberty and independence. To that end," said Calhoun, "let us then bind the republic together with a perfect system of roads and canals, bring the country farmer into the network of the market system, and make the country price approximate to that of the commercial towns." If the subsistence surplus farmer in the hinterlands of Massachusetts complained against Calhoun's proposal, that he start producing for distant national and world markets instead of working for himself and his household, Calhoun would scold back against the fatal weakness of human nature that chooses "ease and pleasure over labor and virtue."

With Henry Clay as Speaker of the House of Representatives, Calhoun became the floor leader for the National Republican agenda, and one by one he and Clay piloted the new legislation through the turbulent waters of the House; there was more than enough political turbulence to keep them busy, too.

In the House of Representatives, the charter for the second Bank of the United States squeaked past old-guard Republican opposition by a margin of only nine votes, 80 to 71. The new taxes and tariffs got by with a 31-vote margin, but that was largely because of the lopsided support they received from the northern states, which would directly benefit from the tariffs. The transportation bill brought on debate and wrangling that lasted until March of 1817, and then President Madison lost his nerve in the face of so much Republican opposition and vetoed the bill.

As Madison came to the end of his second term, the Republican caucus in Congress decided that it wanted to be very careful about choosing for its candidate a successor who would be safe, and so, as their candidate for the 1816 presidential election, they turned to James Monroe. Monroe was safe, or at least they thought he was safe. Like Clay and Calhoun, Monroe had been appalled at the failure of the Republican ideology to carry the United States to victory in the War of 1812, and what was even more persuasive, Monroe was already seriously in debt himself to John Jacob Astor, and would become even more deeply enmeshed in debt to the second bank.

Monroe hardly had a choice but to announce his support for the second bank, and what was more, he launched a second war against the Barbary pirates, largely to justify continuing the navy building program. He also threw his weight entirely behind Calhoun's designs for a perfect system of roads and canals.

Well, there would have been very little point to this agenda. There would have been very little point in the National Republicans' efforts to protect domestic manufacturing, build up the national credit system, and move American agriculture onto the markets of the world, unless there was a workable system of national transportation to get it there, and that simply wasn't available in America in 1816. I mean, an ordinary stagecoach ride from Boston to New York cost between 10 and 11 dollars in 1820. That's 1820 dollars. That's two days' wages, and that said nothing for the cost of shipping produce or driving cattle to market. Five weeks were needed to move a stagecoach from Nashville, Tennessee, to Washington City.

These costly and unpleasant facts were what lay behind Calhoun's promotion of the bank, because he saw the bank as the mechanism for funding the building of a national road system beginning in the East at Cumberland, Maryland, and stretching all the way West to the Mississippi at St. Louis. Construction on a Cumberland Road project had actually begun in 1811, and by 1817 the road had crept out to Wheeling, Virginia, on the Ohio River, but President Madison, in the closing days of his administration, was too overcome by his doubts about the road's constitutionality to give any further endorsement. What the federal government could not do the state governments could, though.

The cheapest and most obvious means of state-funded transportation was the construction of turnpikes. The first private turnpike system had been built in 1794 in Pennsylvania by Robert Morris, and it linked Lancaster and Philadelphia. By 1810, New York corporations had built over 1,000 miles of turnpikes, and 4,000 miles by 1820, more than twice the mileage of any other state, but even with the renewed frenzy of road building, the turnpikes would never be more than an extension of 18th-century modes of travel. It was at this moment that 19th-century ingenuity provided an answer in the form of the steamboat.

Now, the use of steam as a means of providing mechanical power was actually developed in the early 1700s in Britain, by Thomas Newcombe, but an American inventor, John Fitch, experimented in 1787 with the possibility of mounting a steam engine on a barge and letting the engine power a paddle wheel at the barge's stern. Fitch's barge, however, was too poorly designed to make him money, and Fitch eventually migrated to France to try his hand at persuading the new French Republic to invest in steamboats.

In August of 1807, another Pennsylvania inventor, Robert Fulton, launched another steamboat on the Hudson River. Unlike the luckless John Fitch, Robert Fulton was both a better builder and had better financial backing from the powerful Livingston clan of New York—he got that money because, quite prudently, Robert Fulton married one of the Livingstons in 1808.

The North River steamboat of *Claremont*, as Fulton named his creation, might have looked, as it was described by one person, "precisely like a backwoods sawmill mounted on a scow and set on fire," but it drove 150 miles upriver from New York City to Albany in only 32 hours. Talk about speed. Within a month after the *Claremont's* trial run, she was carrying 90 passengers per trip. Robert Fulton died in 1815, but he had already foreseen that steamboats could easily turn every navigable river in the United States into a fast, cheap highway.

In 1811, a flat-bottomed, shallow-draft steamboat of only 371 tons' weight was built by a group of Pittsburgh investors and optimistically named *New Orleans*. Sent down the Ohio and the Mississippi to its namesake city, the *New Orleans* easily beat the transportation time required for flatboats on the Mississippi, and by 1815 the steamboat *Enterprise* was making the upriver trip from New Orleans to Louisville in only 25 days. A decade later, the time had been cut to under a week.

By 1820, there were 31 steamboats operating on the Mississippi and Ohio Rivers. Five years later, there were 75. Ten years after that, there were 361 steamboats on the Mississippi and on all of its various tributaries—the Wabash, the Monongahela, the Tennessee, the Missouri, the Cumberland, and the Arkansas. Before steam, it had cost $5 to move 100 pounds of freight by river between New Orleans and Louisville. By 1830, the steamboats had cut back to $2, and over the next 20 years it fell to only 25 cents. The only restraint the steamboats seemed to suffer was the fact that they could go only where natural waterways would permit them to go, but if a river did not flow someplace naturally, make one flow artificially, and thus the great canal mania was born.

Canals, like turnpikes, had been constructed by states and by private entrepreneurs as a transportation solution all during the first three decades of the republic's existence, but also, like the early turnpikes, they had been small-scale affairs, none of them longer than 28 miles and probably amounting to no more than a total of about 100 miles throughout the country.

Then, in 1817, the new Republican governor of New York, DeWitt Clinton, floated a risky state bond issue for over, hold your breath, seven million dollars, to finance a gigantic canal across the length of upper New York state from Buffalo on Lake Erie to Albany on the Hudson, thus bringing the rural agricultural resources of northern New York into the grasp of the New York City markets. I cannot tell you what a breathtaking gamble this was. There was no precedent for an engineering project this mammoth anywhere in the world, and there were no engineers in America capable of designing it.

In fact, the canal was surveyed and dug by two New York lawyers, who not only learned engineering on the job, but who also, in the process, invented excavating machines and stump pullers as they went. Jefferson decried the canal as "little short of madness," and Clinton's political enemies sneered at the canal as "Clinton's big ditch," but after 363 miles and seven years, the Erie Canal was triumphantly opened on November 2, 1825, with a canal boat procession along the length of the canal and a gala celebration in New York City, where DeWitt Clinton poured a keg of Lake Erie water into the Atlantic Ocean.

Cut four feet deep and 40 feet wide, over 18 aqueducts and through 38 lochs that raised the water level a total of 568 feet between Albany and Buffalo, the canal had been a political godsend for Clinton, creating thousands of public-works jobs for the canal workers who, of course, happily reelected Governor Clinton as governor of New York in 1825, but even more the Erie Canal altered the economic complexion of the northeastern United States at one stroke. Freight between Albany and Buffalo, which had cost $100 a ton and 15 to 45 days to be hauled by wagon, now cost only six dollars a ton by canal boat, and took only nine days to make the trip.

Nor were the profits limited to the canal's users only. Tiny villages on the canal's route, like Syracuse and Rochester became boom towns for servicing goods and for moving traffic, while the tolls paid by the canal boats netted 42 million dollars for the state treasury over the next 60 years. The spectacular success of the Erie Canal set off a rash of canal building across the states, but in the same year that the Erie Canal opened, yet another transportation innovation made a debut that in fact would render canals obsolete. This was the railroad or, to be more accurate, the steam-powered locomotive engine. The British had been working to develop steam-powered railroad service since 1821, and in September of 1825, 40,000 people watched the steam-powered engine, locomotion, make the first commercial run on the eight-and-a-half-mile-long Stockton & Darlington Railroad.

American entrepreneurs and engineers lost no time in following suit. In the same year, Colonel John Stevens, a wealthy tinkerer, built a small steam-power locomotive that ran on a circular track, which Stevens built on his summer estate at Hoboken, New Jersey. The first commercial rail line began construction on July 4, 1828, with the laying of the first rail of what would become the 73-mile track of the Baltimore & Ohio Railroad.

Two years later, with the rail line complete, a former brewer and brickmaker named Peter Cooper put his own locomotive, *Tom Thumb*, on the Baltimore & Ohio line and hauled the first load of 30 passengers around Baltimore. Within 10 years, there was more railroad mileage in the United States than canal mileage, and over the next 20 years the railroads grew to cover 30,626 miles of track.

Now, taking canals, turnpikes, steamboats, and railroads together, the cost of transporting goods on land in the United States fell by 95 percent between 1825 and 1855. Ninety-five percent. That's how much the cost of moving goods fell in the midst of this great revolution in transportation, and the speed of carrying those goods accelerated fivefold, but even more important was the dramatic way in which this revolution in transportation permitted the long fingers of the market to reach into what had once been the remote agrarian societies of independent patriarchal farmers.

As the costs of bringing market-produced imports into the rural hinterlands fell—as it was now cheaper to bring outside goods, and easier to bring outside goods, into the various remote districts of the republic—farm households began to abandon their traditional household manufacture of shoes, cloth, and other goods in order to buy cheaply priced textiles and fancy manufactured goods. In western Massachusetts, between 1815 and 1830, households stopped spinning wool yarn and flax for their own use, and began buying and wearing inexpensive store-bought clothing. To pay for their increasing dependence on those goods, farmers were forced to tease larger and more productive harvests out of their soils, employ cost-saving machinery, and eventually turn to single-crop agriculture in which they produced exclusive harvests of corn or wheat for distant and invisible markets.

Even the merchants themselves changed. By 1845, most of the goods in the stores of western Massachusetts merchants were not the local-grown, local-manufactured goods that you might have found 20 years before. Oh, no, no, no. By the 1840s, the goods in the stores of western Massachusetts merchants were all coming from New York City suppliers. Not only was the market changing the economic world of Thomas Jefferson's farmers, it was also changing its social spirit—its social ethos. The greater the distance involved in selling agricultural goods to these markets, the more farmers were forced to turn to borrowing on distant credit markets and to the impersonal and abstract form of cash exchange.

As a result, the spirit of face-to-face social reciprocity wilted. By the 1830s, the number of mortgages on farm properties in western Massachusetts had doubled, and as indebtedness on property increased, so did the number of lawsuits over those debts brought by merchants against farmers.

It was not the merchants, of course. It was the market itself that was changing traditional rural ways of life. As one writer bitterly commented in a New England agricultural newspaper in 1829, "The market is a canker that will by degrees eat you out while you are eating upon it." In fact, farmers were not the only ones impacted by the penetration of world markets into the American economy. Following the lead of the federal government in chartering the second Bank of the United States, new banks sprang up on state-issued charters after 1815 like mushrooms overnight.

Over 200 state banks were chartered in 1815 alone, with another 392 bank charters being issued over the next three years. These banks, in turn, stashed their specie deposits, the gold and silver that was supposed to be the basis of their business, in their vaults and—against those specie deposits—they issued such a flood of paper bank notes that the overall American money supply tripled between 1800 and 1830, and what was more, corporations not only borrowed from the banks, not only borrowed from British lenders across the ocean, they also borrowed from the American public in the form of selling stocks and bonds in their corporations.

By 1817, a whole new financial profession, stockbrokering, had appeared in New York City, and New Yorkers had organized the first informal American Stock Exchange on Wall Street. From the viewpoint of someone like President Monroe, the economic anxieties by the penetration of commercial capitalism were more than outweighed by the prosperity that commercial growth lent to the country. I mean, much as Monroe doubted the strict constitutionality of providing public financing for national transportation, after all, this was not of the enumerated powers reserved to the federal government by the Constitution; still, Monroe was happy to recommend a constitutional amendment that would grant such a power. He quietly authorized John Calhoun, whom he had selected as his secretary of war, to use the army engineers to begin surveying likely sites for roads and canals against the day when that constitutional amendment, or the composition of Congress, would permit the federal government to put even more investment into transportation.

At length, even die-hard Federalists conceded their admiration for Monroe's determination to make the United States a great—rather than a small—power, and he had such applause from both Federalists and his own party, the Republicans, that his admirers began to hail the death of party factionalism in America, and to dub Monroe's presidency as *The Era of Good Feelings*.

Thomas Jefferson, now in his 70s and in retirement at Monticello, entertained anything but good feelings for Monroe, for Clay, and for Calhoun. Instead, Jefferson looked on the new post-War of 1812 world as a betrayal of Republican principles. "The bankers have made us believe," Jefferson complained, "that legerdemain tricks upon paper," like stock certificates, paper bank notes, "can produce as solid wealth as hard labor in the earth. The result," Jefferson prophesied, "can only be a general demoralization of the nation, a filching from industry of its honest earnings, wherewith to build up palaces and raise gambling stock for swindlers and shavers who are to close their career of piracies by fraudulent bankruptcies." Never mind, of course, that Thomas Jefferson himself personally— literally—had never worked in the earth. That had been a task that he delegated to his slaves. Nevertheless, Jefferson believed that now was the time. Now was perhaps, in fact, the last chance to strike back, and to ensure that his "revolution of 1800" had not been for nothing.

Lecture Twenty-Three
A Nation Announcing Itself

Scope:

Lafayette's visit for the 50th anniversary of the Revolution and the passing of both Jefferson and Adams on July 4, 1826, were landmarks in the progress of the republic. By the 1820s, rural households in Massachusetts were no longer the self-sufficient, independent economic worlds they had once been; immigrants flowed through America's seaports from Europe; and with the clearance of Indian resistance, the Northwest Territory was opened by massive government land sales. Many emigrants chose to stay in the cities they first entered, and their numbers soon swelled the size of the American urban population. The result was an ever-increasing imbalance in the distribution of wealth in the new cities of the republic, especially for free urban black Americans. The disorienting physical symbols of the new western land, and the even more disorienting reality of being thrown together with new people, created what Alexis de Tocqueville called "a perpetual instability in the men and in the laws."

Outline

I. The 50th anniversary of American independence marked a turning point for the republic.

    A. The anniversary marked the passing of the revolutionary generation.

        1. The Marquis de Lafayette made a state visit in 1824–1825.

        2. The Bunker Hill Monument was dedicated in 1825.

        3. John Adams and Thomas Jefferson both died on July 4, 1826.

    B. The anniversary also highlighted changes in American demography.

        1. Between 1790 and 1820, the American population more than doubled.

        2. Although domestic birth rates declined, the decline was more than offset by immigration from Europe.

        3. English-speaking emigrants amounted to 500,000 by 1840.

C. The anniversary pointed to immense geographical growth.
1. The end of the War of 1812 led to tremendous sales of public lands.
2. Most of this went to land speculators.
3. Congress constantly lowered the restrictions to allow greater access to land purchases, but many simply "squatted' and claimed title preemption.
4. The speculators were disliked but were crucial to land development.

II. The most unsettling development was the growth of American cities.

A. Although predominantly agricultural, the United States saw a significant upswing in urban population.
1. Between 1820 and 1850, the number of cities with more than 5,000 inhabitants rose from 12 to 150.
2. Existing cities became denser.
3. Many western pioneers went, not to farm, but to build cities in the interior.

B. Cities were the economic nerve centers of the republic.
1. Home-based manufacturing yielded to the factory system.
2. The imbalance of wealth distribution became acute.

C. In theory, urban laborers had an "escape valve" available in western lands.
1. That was not true for urban free blacks.
2. White migrants discovered flimsiness and instability.

D. The ultimate casualty of these developments was republicanism.
1. Republicanism feared a society built on self-interest rather than virtue.
2. In the West and in the cities, self-interest reigned supreme.
3. This signaled the conversion of republicanism into democracy.

Essential Reading:

Faragher, *Sugar Creek.*

Supplementary Reading:

Smith, *The "Lower Sort": Philadelphia's Laboring People.*

Tocqueville, *Democracy in America.*

Questions to Consider:

1. Does the sale of federal lands constitute a governmental "intervention" in the economy?

2. How is democracy different from republicanism?

Lecture Twenty-Three—Transcript
A Nation Announcing Itself

The year 1824 brought to a close the last term of James Monroe as president, and set off plans for celebrations throughout 1825 of the 50th anniversary of the beginning of the American Revolution. Only a handful of the revolutionary leaders were still alive by then. Washington had died in 1799, three years after leaving the presidency; Hamilton was dead from Aaron Burr's pistol in 1804. Paul Revere of the famous Midnight Ride had died in 1818, and even King George III was gone at last, dying in 1820. Thomas Jefferson and John Adams were still alive, in their 80s, and (from France) Monroe had arranged to bring the 68-year-old Marquis de Lafayette—the last surviving major general of the Revolution—to America for a state visit. The visit was a smashing success.

Lafayette, who had come as a youthful French volunteer to serve on Washington's staff during the Revolution, was as vain and charming as he'd ever been; from city-to-city and town-to-town, he was treated to banquets, outdoor fireworks, and performances. He paid calls on Adams and Jefferson, and he capped it all off by presiding at the dedication ceremonies on June 17, 1825, of the monument at Bunker Hill, across the Charles River from Boston. Then, it was over; Lafayette departed aboard the steamship *Mount Vernon* in July, never to return to the nation he had fought for, and where he was an honorary citizen. One year later, Thomas Jefferson died at Monticello. In the last 13 years of his life, Jefferson had managed to patch up the quarrel he had picked with John Adams over Federalism and the Alien and Sedition Acts, and the two old political veterans of the Revolution had begun a kind of old cronies' correspondence on subjects that ranged from religion to foreign affairs.

Adams was weakening, and weakening fast, in the winter of 1825-1826, though, and three hours after Jefferson's death on July 4, 1826, the 50th anniversary of the Declaration of Independence, John Adams died as well. His last words had an ironic, although mistaken satisfaction to them. He said "Thomas Jefferson still lives." Lafayette's visit for the 50th anniversary of the Revolution, and the passing of both Jefferson and Adams on July 4, 1826, were landmarks in the progress of the republic. They were an unmistakable reminder of the disappearance of the revolutionary generation, and with it, how much the American republic had changed since the days of the Revolution. The most obvious change in the first 50 years of the republic was its sheer numerical growth. The first federal census in 1790 had found fewer than four million people in the United States; by 1820 that number had surpassed nine million; by 1850 it would increase even more dramatically to 23 million. Now, most of that growth was due at first to simple natural increase; women who married in 1780 and 1789 in rural Massachusetts usually did so at aged 23 or 24 and could expect seven or eight live births during their childbearing years. After 1800, this high rate of births began to fall off as the age at marriage rose to 25 and the number of expected live births fell to six. After 1810, the birth rate fell even more dramatically, so that by the 1830s women in rural Massachusetts usually had—on average—only four children.

Whatever falling off the American population felt from the decrease in American birthrates was more than made up for by the ever-swelling number of emigrants flowing through American seaports from Europe. This immigration was part of an immense movement of European peoples out of Europe in the 19th century, all across the globe, but between 1815 and 1840 it was especially a movement of people out of the British Isles. Part of the reason for this movement was demographic; although European birth rates fell in the 1800s from what they'd been a century before, European death rates fell even faster as the medical advances of the 1700s caught up with the general population. The result was that the British population jumped from 10 million in 1800 to over 26 million by 1870, even though it was hemorrhaging emigrants at a fearful rate. This alarming increase in the size of the British population occurred at precisely the same moment as British capitalism was shifting from a commercial mode to an industrial mode, driving people off the farmlands they'd tilled for generations, and into the already overcrowded cities where work was precarious and life often unbearable.

By 1830, 6,000 Scottish farmers were being forced out of the highlands every year and by 1832 50,000 Protestant and Catholic Irish from British-ruled Ireland were on their way to America. For those who did manage to survive in the countryside, there was the burden of taxation, as the British government sought to pay off the immense debts it had contracted during the Napoleonic Wars.

As if taxation weren't enough, the European winters between 1825 and 1829 were horrendously cold and trigged famines and food shortages in Ireland and Germany. Now by contrast to all of this, America offered the prospect of abundant cheap land in a republic where there was no military draft, no censorship, no political police, no aristocrats, and taxation rates that stood at only one-tenth of those of Great Britain. The English-speaking emigrants kept on coming—50,000 of them in 1816, when the ending of the Napoleonic Wars made large-scale immigration possible again across the North Atlantic—300,000 of them arrived in the 1830s.

By 1840, over a total of some 500,000 English-speaking emigrants had come to the United States. In an age in which the English-speaking emigrant needed no passport, no health certificate, and in fact really didn't need much else apart from the £10 or £12 for the cost of passage; what this meant was that anybody who survived the two to four week voyage across the North Atlantic could step off the boat in New York or in Philadelphia without anybody enquiring who they were, or where they intended to go, or what they intended to do.

These emigrants might have attracted more attention and more resentment if, once off the boat, they had had nowhere to go but the port cities of the United States, but the transportation revolution that had so dramatically dropped the cost of moving goods also cheapened the cost of moving people, and so the emigrants quickly fanned out along the network of canals and rivers that led to the great heartland beyond the Appalachian Mountains. What's more, the end of the War of 1812 also meant the end of Indian resistance.

One thing that might have contained the spread on a large-scale of emigrants in the trans-Appalachia West would have been active Indian resistance, but as the War of 1812 came to an end and Indian resistance in the northern woodlands disintegrated, Tecumseh was killed, and Andrew Jackson's conquest of the Red Sticks smashed Indian resistance in the South. All of this allowed the federal government to clear off the Indian tribes from the land east of the Mississippi almost as easily and directly as the lords and ladies and factories were clearing off farmers in Scotland and Ireland. What it really meant was that there were now huge areas, huge tracts of territory, open and available for the developing, without the personal threat of Indian resistance.

In 1815, the federal government sold off one and one-third million acres of western land; in 1818, it sold off another three million acres. That's something equivalent to the entire state of Connecticut, from what had once been Indian-occupied territory. Now mind you, I've said that emigrants could step off the boat, step onto the canal, get across the Appalachians, and suddenly find themselves without any threat to developing land. Now, that land on the other side of the Appalachians, please do not make the mistake of assuming that all that land was available for an emigrant with a little bit of cash. Most of the land that the federal government owned on the other side of the Appalachian Mountains, owned whether it was because of the original deed at the end of the Treaty of Paris in which the British had deeded over to America, and in this case, Congress, over to the government all the title to that land or that which was possessed by the United States after evicting the Indian tribes—all that land wasn't going to be sold easily or piece-by-piece just to emigrants; most of it in fact was sold first at least to land speculators.

Federal laws dating all the way back to the North West Ordinance in 1787 mandated the sale of land, in this case federally owned land; the North West Ordinance mandated those sales in sections of 640 acres. This was to be sold at two dollars an acre. That certainly is cheap enough; however, when you have to buy it in a block of 640 acres, that's beyond the capacities of most individuals to buy much less to farm effectively. I don't know how effective a farmer you might be but 640 acres is pretty daunting even in modern times.

On the other hand, land speculators who had cash in hand—or who had the cash of investors in their company in hand—willingly bought up the 640-acre sections of land, then subdivided them and sold the land to individual settlers or emigrants in smaller parcels, of course at considerable profit. This set off a land purchase bonanza. Congress fuelled this bonanza still further in 1819 when, in an effort to cut the speculators out of the process and ease the impact of the Panic of 1819, Congress dropped the price of federally owned land from two dollars an acre to one dollar and 25 cents an acre, wiped out interest charges on land purchases, and reduced the minimum purchase lot to 80 acres; even then people clamored for better deals, though.

They not only clamored for better deals, but went out and got them by main force; many settlers by-passed the process of purchase entirely and simply crossed the Appalachians and "squatted" on federal lands, hoping to make good their title to the land by the simple fact of possession. By the end of 1828, two-thirds of the population of Illinois was squatters, and in 1841, Congress yielded to their pressure and legitimized their titles by the process of "preemption." Preemption was a means by which a squatter could buy out the title to up to 180 acres of land in his use, though it can't really be called possession, but the up to 180 acres that that squatter was actually farming could be purchased retroactively at the Congress price of one dollar and 25 cents an acre.

This, despite the fact that the squatter having squatted there for a number of years had improved the land, with everyone else all around improving the land. The actual value of that land had gone through the roof, but preemption allowed the squatter to purchase the land at the Congress price—the old, very inexpensive price that had been set by Congress. That was what squatting got you, and in the case of Illinois and most of the other western lands it got you a great deal.

Now, the classic image of this process of occupation of the trans-Appalachian heartland is usually the "Daniel Boone, Davey Crockett" hero—the restless, fighting Anglo-American male with an axe on one shoulder and a rifle on the other. The most critical people in the settlement of the western lands were really the land speculators, though, not the pioneers. It was the land speculators who settled the trans-Appalachian interior not with axes and rifles, but with surveying tools and with financial savvy.

Even after the abolition of the 640-acre block sales, land sales still required middle men to organize the sales and to act as go-betweens for the new waves of emigrants. Moses Cleveland—who was the agent for the Connecticut land company—never swung an axe in his life that we know of, but by organizing sales of land in an immense tract on Lake Eerie in Northern Ohio at a dollar an acre and on five years' credit, he laid the foundations for the village and then the city that today bears his name.

Land speculators like Moses Cleveland may have been particularly successful in financial terms, but that doesn't mean that they were particularly popular, especially with the squatters. The squatters frequently planted themselves on land owned by speculators. I mean, the process would be like this: A squatter would come in squat on federally owned land, only to discover that that federally owned land wasn't owned by the federal government any more; it had been bought up by a speculator—it had been bought up by a land company.

When the squatter demanded title to that land by right of possession at the Congress price, which of course the land speculators didn't want to sell the land for because it was too inexpensive and would have made their work and their intervention ridiculous, at that point rows between the squatters and the speculators could be spectacular and violent—but all the same, the speculators, whether they liked it or not, were indispensable. They built up the towns of the heartland; they formed the lobbies behind the National Republican program for roads and internal improvements; they took most of the financial risks in development; and in the end, they may have served better purposes than anyone dreamed.

Let me explain: The constant pressure on Congress to cheapen the price of land encouraged settlers to buy as much land as they had credit or cash for, and with prices as cheap as one dollar and 25 cents an acre, settlers might easily buy up far more land than they had any realistic hope of farming or improving. Well, with land cheap but the labor to work it very, very dear the temptation would become irresistible to open up sources of slave labor to work that land, thus pressuring Congress to reopen the African slave trade.

Now, by contrast, the speculators, by buying up land and having bought it, developing it and forcing the price of land upwards, forced settlers to buy only what was manageable with their own labor, and so the speculators actually exerted an invisible restraint on the further spread of slavery in the American republic. Doubtless, they never set out to perform that service, but perform it they did.

Even with the availability of western land in all of these different forms and packages, not all emigrants chose to go West; many of them really did stay in the cities that they first entered, and their numbers soon swelled the size of the American urban population. Although the United States remained a securely and overwhelmingly rural country through the 1800s, there was still a significant upswing in the size and proportion of the urban population of the United States. The 1820 census showed that the United States had only 12 cities of more than 5,000 souls, but by 1850 there were nearly 150 such cities, and then by 1820, only nine percent of the American population could logically be called urban. By 1850, though, the number had risen to 20 percent.

At the same time the ratio of rural farmers to city dwellers went from 15 to one, 15 farmers to one city dweller in 1800 to 10 farmers to one in 1830. Only someone who works with numbers could come up with half a farmer, but that's what the numbers work out to. Ten to one in 1830, and by 1850 the ratio between rural and urban is down to five to one.

Not only were there more city dwellers, but the cities they dwelt in were becoming denser and more complex. New York City, finally, outstripped Philadelphia with a population of over 500,000 people in 1850. Philadelphia, Boston, and Baltimore counted over 100,000 people apiece, and it wasn't just simply the eastern seacoast cities that experienced this dramatic upsurge of urban population. Emigrants who went west often went there not to settle farms but to build cities in the interior like St. Louis and Cincinnati—which also topped out at over 100,000 people—or New Orleans or Chicago. Chicago sprang up from being originally simply a military outpost, to 4,000 inhabitants in 1830, to over 30,000 in 1850. By the time of the 1850 census more than one-third of the republic's city dwellers lived in cities in the interior of the United States, not on the old colonial coastline.

These cities were the economic nerve centers of the republic, and they revealed sooner than any part of the rest of the country what the social costs of integrating the American republic with the world capitalist markets of Europe might be. The production of manufactured goods in the colonial cities had been small-scale and usually the work of an individual artisan or an individual mechanic who superintended all the aspects of the manufacturing of a product. An example of this is a shoemaker; a shoemaker in one of the old colonial towns would do measuring, do the cutting of the material, do the stitching of the shoes, and of course, all of this would be for individual customers, so all of it was made as custom-made.

Labor and production for distant markets, along with the rush of postwar capital and credit, drove out this kind of domestic manufacturing, where everything was done by one or two people under one roof. In its place came the "putting-out" system and the reduction of the independent artisan to a wage labor man, a wage paid by an entrepreneur or a capitalist who controlled the sources of new materials and kept the profits from the goods, that is the profits after wages for himself. The result was an ever-increasing imbalance in the distribution of wealth in the new cities of the republic. In New York; Brooklyn, which was until the 1890s a separate city from New York City (and don't suggest otherwise to Brooklynites who still guard their identity very carefully, some of whom still really believe that Brooklyn ought to be a separate city from New York City); Boston; and Philadelphia—in those places the top one percent of the list of tax-paying citizens owned almost 25 percent of all the available taxable wealth in 1825, that's one percent owning 25 percent. By 1850, 25 years later, that same one percent at the top of the population of those cities owned over half of the wealth of that city.

At least in theory, the way of escape for poor city wage laborers who determined that this was quite enough, thank you, was westward, to become independent land owners. If you didn't want to be an exploited urban wage earner, you could simply go west, get cheap land, and set yourself up as an independent American farmer. For many urban laborers, even that escape was economically impossible, and for yet another segment of the urban population it wasn't only economically but socially impossible. That segment was the population of free urban black Americans.

In 1860, nearly a quarter of a million free African Americans lived in the northern states of the republic, mostly in the eastern cities, but few free blacks had the right to vote outside New England. Property qualifications disenfranchised all but seven percent of the northern black population, and most of those were forced to use—even in the North—segregated facilities on steamboats, railroads, restaurants, and even in churches. Most free African Americans were also segregated in another way, in that they were confined to the most unskilled and low-paying jobs. In Philadelphia in 1838, 80 percent of the black workers were unskilled, and three out of five black families owned property worth less than 60 dollars.

American blacks struggled to come to terms with being in urban American society, but not being permitted to be of it. Excluded from trade deals and churches, they formed their own self-help associations, even their own religious denominations such as Richard Allen's African Methodist Epistle Zion Church in Philadelphia. In New York City, where as many as one-third of African American heads of households were artisans, black New Yorkers formed their own New York African Society for Mutual Relief, and in 1814, they made a bold gesture for inclusion in the New York City community by volunteering the labor of all free people of color for a day on the city's harbor fortifications to protect the city from British invasion.

Black city dwellers lost the struggle for independence almost as often as they won it, though. "I feel it almost impossible not to despond entirely of there ever being a better day for us," wrote Charlotte Forten, a free black woman in Philadelphia. "None but those who experience it can know what it is, this constant galling sense of cruel injustice and wrong."

In the case of black Americans, there was little or no outlet to the western lands. Ohio, Indiana, and Illinois actually passed laws banning black immigration into those states. For those who were white, male, and sufficiently aggressive, however, the western interior was hardly less than the Promised Land, and so they packed up and went.

The symbols of this breaking up were present everywhere, even in house construction. Americans on the move stopped building the sturdy mortar tannin heavy timbered houses that dotted the old colonial landscapes. In the 1820s, they started building something different—cheap, lightweight balloon-frame houses that could be constructed around light frames of two-by-fours held together by nails, not mortar and tannin, and covered with light boards or cardboards. Not only could balloon frames be constructed quickly and by fewer hands, but they could be knocked down and moved as the people moved. St. Mary's Church in Chicago was built on the balloon-frame model and was knocked down, moved, and rebuilt three times in the first 10 years of its existence during the 1830s.

A society can't be taken apart and rebuilt with quite the ease of a house. Societies are built out of intangible glue like trust, like shared unspoken assumptions, like recognition of places and orders, however you sought them out. A nation in motion put trust in jeopardy, and so it is no surprise that at this time we begin to find the rise of stories, self-help manuals, and tales about swindlers in the new republic, like Herman Melville's *The Confidence Man*, because in the jumble of immigration westward, no one knew who anyone else was, nobody knew whom they could trust, and there could be no sense of order or place in a society where no one knew what order you represented or what place you came from. If you did have all those things, you soon learned that you didn't matter at all.

It didn't matter where you were born or where you came from, so the real casualty of the helter-skelter settlement of the West was republicanism itself. After all, republicanism had no more use for raw individualism than it did for aristocracy. Classical republicans, and this included Jefferson and Hamilton alike, feared a society built solely upon the pursuit of individual interests, because they knew how easily the unbridled pursuit of individual interests would lead to massive inequality; then inequality would lead to political corruption and tyranny. Both Jefferson and Hamilton believed that liberty and commerce had to be counter-posed by the cultivation of selfless disinterested virtue; that quality, both Jefferson and Hamilton knew, required training, discipline, and stability—three qualities that life in the West had no use for.

In the West, land wasn't a mystic symbol of righteousness or status, it was a commodity to be bought or sold, and in some cases simply squatted on. The jumble of speculators, squatters, and emigrants in the West represented precisely the free wheeling pursuit of self-interest and the abandonment of disinterested virtue that Jefferson and Hamilton dreaded. It signaled the slow effacement of classical republicanism by a new conception of political society, where the interest of the individual was the paramount consideration, and each individual voice was as good as any other in determining policy. That new form of political organization is what we call "democracy," or to be more accurate, it signaled the end of the republican ideology that Jefferson believed had been restored to permanent sway in his "revolution of 1800."

That republican ideology would now begin to splinter, and the veil of traditional republicanism would begin to tear into two sections. Each section would claim to represent the old republicanism even as it changed beyond recognition; each section of the old republican ideology would have its champion to run for the presidency in the 1820s, and all political organization in American life thereafter would fall to one or the other side of this division. One part of this division was already on hand in the person of Henry Clay and the National Republicans who represented the interests of economic growth and development. The other was already taking shape in the backlash against the National Republican agenda and the Panic of 1819. That faction would become the Democrats, and it would find its principle in raw democracy and its champion in Andrew Jackson.

Lecture Twenty-Four
National Republican Follies

Scope:

The year 1819 blew up in the faces of the bankers, brokers, National Republicans, and everyone else who had leveraged themselves to the market system. The next great shock, in 1819, was known as the *Great Panic*. The United States had to learn that committing itself to the world market system exacted a price in the form of the unpredictable cycle of boom and bust. Popular outrage against the legislatures that had permitted this to happen exploded in demands to widen voting rights. Ultimately, the Supreme Court sat squarely in the path of an angered democracy. In 1819, the Supreme Court heard appeals in the cases of *Dartmouth College v. Woodward* and *Sturgis v. Crowninshield* and, in 1824, in *Gibbons v. Ogden*, all of which determined the fault-line between economics and politics in American life.

Outline

I. The National Republicans were not unaware of the risks of market involvement, but they believed it was essential to national greatness.

    A. The rapid rate of American development came to a crashing halt in the economic panic of the year 1819.

    B. The Panic of 1819 began with the state banks.

        1. State banks could not issue coin, but they could issue paper bank notes.

        2. The collapse of British cotton prices set off a run on the state banks.

        3. The state banks and the Second Bank of the United States, in turn, called in loans.

II. The panic generated massive popular unrest.

    A. Debtor relief laws were passed by state legislatures.

        1. Every western legislature adopted measures to postpone foreclosure sales, restricting liquidation sales, closing state courts to creditors, and forcing creditors to accept bank notes.

2. These measures were risky because they were unconstitutional.
B. Banks were closed or outlawed by legislatures.
   1. Some states permitted the establishment only of a state-controlled bank.
   2. Even non-bank corporations became the targets of legislative control.
C. Voter reform admitted thousands of new voters to the franchise by eliminating property qualifications.
   1. Republicanism was suspicious of concentrations of power, even when that power was in the hands of the people.
   2. The economic crisis led to an explosion in demands to widen voting rights to the victims of the panic.
   3. Voter participation now surged from 27 percent in 1824 to 80 percent in 1840.
   4. Presidential nominations began moving out of party caucuses and into national conventions.

III. The principal restraint on this popular backlash was the Supreme Court.
A. Law shifted from concentrating on the regulation of behavior to the protection of property and contract.
   1. Law did this because of its kinship to the capitalist ethic.
   2. Lawyers became the "shock troops" of capitalism.
   3. The principal example of this was John Marshall.
B. The Marshall Court heard appeals in a series of critical cases that restrained popular attacks on corporations and contract.
   1. *Dartmouth College v. Woodward* prevented the state of New Hampshire from interfering in the corporate charter of Dartmouth College.
   2. *Sturgis v. Crowninshield* struck down the New York state bankruptcy laws.
   3. *Gibbons v. Ogden* invoked the Commerce Clause to prevent states from interfering in the competitive operations of the market.
   4. The success of the Marshall Court outraged Jeffersonians, who looked for a candidate to turn the tide against the market and found him in Andrew Jackson.

Essential Reading:

William W. Freehling, *The Road to Disunion*, vol. 1: *Secessionists at Bay*.

Supplementary Reading:

G. Edward White, *The Marshall Court and Cultural Change, 1815–1835*, chapters 8–9.

Questions to Consider:

1. How did the roles of lawyers change from the colonial era to the early republic?

2. Why did the application of Missouri for admission as a slave state trigger a controversy in 1819, but not the applications of Ohio, Mississippi, Indiana, or Alabama?

Lecture Twenty-Four—Transcript
National Republican Follies

Henry Clay was no one's fool, especially when it came to economic issues, and he had no illusions that pushing the United States into the networks of world markets was without risks. He declared, however, that he had closely studied the results of the wars in Europe and in America, and he had learned some lessons by it. As he explained it, "They were lessons which satisfied me that national independence was only to be maintained by national resistance against foreign encroachments, by cherishing the interest of the people, and giving to the whole physical power of the country an interest in the preservation of the nation."

Clay went on to endorse the new military program, to endorse that chain of turnpikes I had talked about last time, the roads and canals from Passamaquoddy to New Orleans, and tariffs. He supported tariffs to effectually protect our manufacturers. Along with Clay, John Calhoun—the self-educated son of a hill country farmer in South Carolina—had come up to the House of Representatives in 1811, just in time to join the Republican hew and cry for war.

Like Clay, however, the War of 1812 revealed to Calhoun all the weak links in the Jeffersonian revolution, where republicanism had spoken for the liberty of the individual farmer, or as in the Virginia and Kentucky Resolutions 20 years before that, the liberties of particular sections of the republic. Calhoun now saw a greater threat to American liberty, like too much individualism, too much sectionalism. In a country so extensive and so various in its interests, what is necessary for the common good may apparently be opposed to the interest of particular sections, Calhoun admitted, but that must be submitted to as the condition of our greatness.

Did it really? Did it really have to be submitted to? In the year 1818, a skeptical editorial writer for the *Richmond Virginia Enquirer* surveyed the new development of banking, congressional road building, and internal improvements, and the gradual movement of the United States into the cash economy of international commercial capitalism. The editorial warned the Virginia farmer against the influence of money in the control of his actions. "Beware," the editorial predicted, "by degrees it grows upon us from little to little, until at length we become intoxicated by its influence and indulge in all its vices insensible to our real situation."

As if to provide all the proof that the *Enquirer* and its Jeffersonian readers needed for that warning, the year 1819 promptly blew up in the faces of the bankers, brokers, National Republicans, Henry Clay, John Calhoun, and everyone else who had leveraged themselves to the market system. The Panic of 1819 began with the second Bank of the United States, or if we want to be more specific about this, it began really with the dozens of state-chartered banks that had sprung up in imitation of the second Bank of the United States.

Although the federal government retained its constitutional monopoly on minting official United States gold and silver coin, virtually every other bank—from the second Bank right down to the lowliest state bank—was free to circulate its own paper bank notes. These bank notes were the IOUs that it issued against the security these banks were supposed to have in the form of gold and silver specie in their vaults.

Well, in the great post-War of 1812 development binge, it was all too easy for banks to print bank notes and extend credit far beyond their reserves of specie, and to let something happen that would cause the holders of bank notes to run on the banks and try to cash in their bank notes for hard coin. Then, those banks could easily find themselves ruined in a few days, their vaults empty of gold and silver.

In 1819, that is precisely what happened. The British cotton market—well glutted with more than 10 years of high intensity southern cotton exports, exports from India—lost its steam, and cotton prices promptly fell from a high of 33 cents per pound to 14 cents. That drop—and a colossal drop it was—in cotton income, more than 50 percent, meant that southern merchants couldn't meet their obligations, couldn't pay their debts except with paper money. British merchants began refusing to accept anything from American merchants and American cotton factors but specie, hard coin. At that point, the holders of bank notes turned to their friendly local banks that had issued the notes, and demanded gold or silver, because that was the only thing that the British sources, and the British merchants, and the British factors would accept.

That created a run on state banks as the holders of the bank notes queued up in long lines to turn in their bank notes for the specie they needed. The state banks then moved to defend themselves by foreclosing mortgages and calling in loans, but demanding that the mortgages and loans be paid for in specie because specie was what they needed to pay off the holders of their bank notes. If the money had been lent out or the credit extended to people who could not repay, then the banks were forced to turn to the holders of the bank notes and say, "Sorry." Many of the state banks were themselves wiped out when the second Bank of the United States began defending itself by calling in the loans it had made to the state banks and demanding repayment of those loans in specie to itself. A great fall of economic dominoes began.

"The banking bubbles are breaking," wrote John Quincy Adams on May 27, 1819. "The merchants are crumbling in ruin." Oh, they were, indeed. "The manufacturers are perishing, agriculture stagnating, and distress universal in every part of the country." He was putting it mildly. In Philadelphia, three quarters of the wage-earning labor force was thrown out of work, and over 1,800 people were jailed for unpaid debts. New York City had 13,000 paupers roaming its streets, and small towns in the East faced the prospect of families naked, children freezing in the winter storm, and the fathers without coats and shoes to enable them to work.

That was in the East. Affairs in the West, where the second Bank of the United States was heavily committed to property development, were hit just as badly. The second Bank of the United States, which owned title—literally—to almost half of Cincinnati, foreclosed mortgages and sold off land at less than half its pre-1819 value in order to get specie. Even worse was the personal impact on people. Fifteen thousand lawsuits for debt were begun in Pennsylvania in 1819—500 in a single term of the county court in Nashville, Tennessee. "All the flourishing cities of the West are mortgaged to this money power," wailed Missouri's new senator, Thomas Hart Benton. "They are in the jaws of the monster." Some monster.

"The nation that builds on manufacturers sleeps on gunpowder," wrote the English essayist Robert Southey in 1817, and the gunpowder had now gone off with an unanticipated bang. If, as the National Republicans demanded, the United States was to commit itself to the world market system as a step toward greatness, then there was going to be a price to be paid in the form of the unpredictable cycle of boom and bust, expansion and contraction, which economists in the early 1800s were only just beginning to realize was a permanent feature of commercial capitalism. If so, then the National Republicans, Henry Clay in particular, were now going to have to face the anger of outraged constituents in the republic who decided in the midst of the Panic of 1819 that Thomas Jefferson had been right all along.

John C. Calhoun anxiously told John Quincy Adams that the panic had aroused a general mass of disaffection to the government, not concentrated in any particular direction, but ready to seize upon any event and looking out anywhere for a leader. It was a vague but wide discontent caused by the disordered circumstances of individuals, but resulting in a general impression that there was something radically wrong in the administration of the government. That disaffection took four basic shapes in 1819 and 1820.

The first of those shapes was the pressure to pass debtor relief laws. Every western legislature, except Louisiana and Mississippi, stepped in to rescue hard-pressed farmers and manufacturers by passing debtor relief laws. Now, these laws were legally risky because the federal Constitution specifically forbids the states from passing any law impairing the obligation of contracts. That's in Article I, Section 10. Debtor relief laws, certainly, if they did anything, impaired contracts by intervening in the obligations owed by one person to another.

Nevertheless, the western legislatures found ways around the Constitution. Their debtor relief laws would, for instance, postpone the sales of foreclosed properties for up to two years. They wouldn't try to diminish contract or interfere with the contract or the contracting parties; they would simply put the whole process in the freezer for up to two years. Or, and here was another twist on constitutionalizing debtor relief laws: They would allow sheriffs' sales of seized property only if the liquidation of the property brought at least two-thirds of the original value of the property as decided by a jury of a debtor's neighbors.

Well, of course, in that case, since the debtor's neighbors were going to be the ones making the judgment, then when you came to one of these sales, whatever was gotten for the property the jury would conclude, "Sorry, doesn't make it to the two-thirds limit; therefore, it's not legal." It's not an interference with contract; it's simply an operating procedure.

Another way that legislatures got around these problems was to close state courts to creditors seeking to recover debts or property. The state court was met by someone from another state trying to collect on a bill, trying to collect on a debt owed by someone in this other state; the state court could find some reason to declare this other person not having standing, or at least not having some legal qualification for beginning that suit in the state where the debtor lived.

Another way of dealing with this too would be to force creditors to accept payment in bank notes rather than specie. Now, if you owe me money, if I have lent money to you at some point, and now I suddenly need it and I go to you and say I want you to pay this debt, I want the money that you owe me, I do not expect for you to pay me, let's say, in cans of soup. It's not what I want. I want the money, not the cans of soup. Well, the same thing applies here. Those who had lent money went to people who, because of the panic, did not have the money to pay off and demanded from them gold and silver, specie, "real" money so to speak.

However, the state courts would step in—or the state legislature would step in—and declare that debts could be paid in paper bank notes, and you would be compelled to accept them or forget trying to collect the debt at all. You'd get no state support behind you; the legislature would not be behind you; the court would not be behind you. The court and the legislature were telling you that even though you didn't want those cans of soup, even though you didn't want those paper bank notes, even if you regarded those paper bank notes as worthless, nevertheless, you would be compelled to accept them rather than requiring gold and specie from the person you'd lent money to. All of this was definitely not in violation of the constitutional prohibition on impairing contract, so debtor relief laws are one way the state legislatures had of responding to the Panic of 1819.

Another way of responding to it was to close the banks. Since the banks and their worthless paper cash were seen as the cause of this misery, well, banks came up for violent public attack. Steven Simpson, the editor of Philadelphia's long time Republican newspaper the *Aurora*, called for the total prostration of the banking and funding system by the cancellation of all bank charters. All bank charters. William Henry Harrison, the hero of Tippecanoe, was nearly beaten out in his run for the Ohio state senate only by promising to destroy all banks and to replace all paper money with gold and silver coin, and that despite the fact that Harrison himself was a bank director. The new state constitution from Missouri permitted the establishment of only one state bank within its borders to be partly owned and controlled by the state itself.

The governor of Kentucky, John Adair, called for a constitutional amendment to outlaw banks throughout the nation. Adair sponsored the repeal of the state charters of all banks but the Bank of the Commonwealth of Kentucky, and then used the Bank of the Commonwealth to issue three million dollars in paper currencies, which creditors were then forced by state law to accept in settlement of debts whether it had any value or not.

The rage against corporate charters for banks even touched non-banking corporations. I mean, non-banking corporations failed like banks failed, and those failures left their investors just as penniless as the investors in banks. This resulted in a rash of state laws appearing that gave legislators control over corporate charters.

A third way of dealing with the fallout from the panic was by voter reform. Jefferson and Hamilton alike had thought of themselves as republicans, with a small "R," but not democrats, with a small "D." They believed that government should be kept out of the hands of aristocrats, because aristocracy concentrates too much power for safety and for virtue. On the other hand, neither Jefferson nor Hamilton believed that turning government into outright democracy, with all questions and all power to be decided by popular majorities, would preserve virtue either, since unwashed majorities could be as easily—if not more so—corrupted than tiny aristocratic elites.

For that reason, the elections of presidents of the United States up through Monroe were settled by the votes of the states and the electoral college, not by popular majority. Electors in the college, and even senators in the national Senate, were elected by state legislators, and the right to vote in state elections was severely hedged in by racial, gender, and property qualifications.

With the Panic of 1819, however, popular outrage against the legislatures that had chartered the banks in the first place, and against the Congress, which had created this monster second Bank, exploded in demands to widen voting rights and give the victims of the panic a say in correcting it.

Property qualifications as voting qualifications fell first. In 1821, New York abolished the last vestiges of property qualifications. Any white male who held fee simple property or who paid taxes, had served in the militia, or who had even worked on the public roads, could vote. By 1824, only Virginia, North Carolina, Rhode Island, and Louisiana maintained any kind of significant property qualifications for voting.

Not only did new voting rights widen the number of voters, but the percentage of voters who actually voted also increased. I mean, we know from looking at our own most recent election statistics that you can have a large number of registered voters, but only a small percentage of those who actually vote.

Well, in this case, both figures marched upwards. Not only the numbers of voters increased, but in fact the percentage of those who actually went out and voted also increased. In New Hampshire, 80 percent of the eligible voters now marched to the polls. In Ohio, the percentages reached 90 percent in 1819, and in Alabama, in the same year, 97 percent of eligible voters turned out and voted. On the national level, the demand for more accountability to the people resulted in soaring percentages of voter turnout for presidential elections—from 27 percent of the adult male white population in 1824 to 80 percent in 1840. This also forced the Republican Party to scrap the old method of nominating presidential candidates, the old method of nominating, in other words, by a party caucus among the Republican congressmen, and it moved presidential nominations first into the state legislatures, and then by the 1840s into national party conventions.

Now, what did this mean? What it meant was that under the pressure of the Panic of 1819, the republic was becoming a democracy. Now, with this kind of power in hand, there should have been very little to prevent state legislatures—and even the national Congress—from saying, "Whoops, we made a big mistake in entirely dismantling the National Republican agenda by breaking up banks, corporations, and charters en masse, and disentangling the United States from the world market."

There was one institution standing as firmly in the way of a democratic backlash in 1819 as it had stood in the way of Jefferson's "revolution of 1800," and that was John Marshall's Supreme Court. Before the American Revolution, law in the English-speaking world had existed as a gentile profession, and it served mainly to enforce norms of communal morality. As commercial capitalism came to be the dominant economic engine of prosperity and growth in the British Empire, though, British and American law stopped being a monitor of behavior and became an arbitrator of contracts.

By the year 1800, law in Massachusetts had become a mechanism for defending property and policing contract relationships rather than punishing Sabbath breakers. The law lent itself so easily to commercial capitalism because in some senses the law was kin to the capitalist ethic. Lawyers in courtrooms adopt a relationship of adversaries to each other—with the best argument, not necessarily the most moral, winning. That is similar to capitalism's use of economic adversaries to come up with the best price for the best goods. Lawyers became, in the memorable phrase of Charles Sellers, the "shock troops" of capitalism in America. Everywhere, they set out to defend the rights of property and the rights of contract against the willful demands of mobs and legislators for equity and the illusive moral quality of fairness.

Everybody wants fairness but nobody quite knows what it is. "Lawyers as a body," wrote the French aristocratic Alexis de Tocqueville who wrote an extended and highly perceptive commentary on American institutions entitled "Democracy in America" in 1830. De Tocqueville said that lawyers form the most powerful, if not the only, counterpoise to the democratic element. "When the American people are intoxicated by their passions or carried away by the impetuosity of their ideas they are checked," said de Tocqueville, "by the almost invisible influence of their legal counselors."

No single lawyer in America embodied that attitude more than the chief justice of the United States, John Marshall, who now placed himself and the Supreme Court squarely in the path of what they regarded as a wild-eyed mob. Marshall had already used the Court's authority to assert the supremacy of the federal judiciary to both Congress and the president. He now used it again to keep the outraged legislatures from smashing the National Republicans to pieces. In 1819, the very year of the panic, Marshall and the Supreme Court heard appeals in the case of *Dartmouth College v. Woodward*. It was a case in which Dartmouth College was protesting an attempt by the New Hampshire legislature to rewrite the college's charter.

Now, the purpose of this rewrite of the charter was to allow the legislature to appoint new trustees. Essentially, what the state legislature wanted to do was to get hold of the charter, and rewrite the charter so that they could seize control of what was—for all practical purposes—a private corporation for the legislature's public purposes, because if they could rewrite the charter and expand the number of trustees, the legislature could appoint its friends to the trustee board of the college, and their votes in trustee meetings would essentially mean that the legislature controlled Dartmouth College. Now this seizing of a private corporation for public purposes was done under the legal umbrella of the legislature's authority to issue charters, so no one would see it at first blush as a seizure of property. However, Dartmouth's defense counsel—a New Hampshire lawyer named Daniel Webster who was taking his first steps onto the national stage—saw that at once and made an eloquent appeal for the independence of Dartmouth. "Dartmouth is," he said, "but a small college, yet there are those who love it."

The real decision in the case was determined not so much by Webster's eloquence, but by Marshall's determination to uphold the untouchability of corporate charters under Article I, Section 10, of the Constitution. Marshall argued that corporate charters constitute contracts. Therefore, Marshall declared in an 18-page opinion upholding Dartmouth College, "under the Constitution no state legislature can meddle with them without violating the constitutional ban on the impairment of contract." No matter what good purposes might have motivated the legislature in dealing with Dartmouth College for attempting to rewrite its charter, that, said Marshall, was a violation of the Constitution, and so by extension would be every other state legislative effort to try to rewrite charters, interfere with charters, interfere with contracts, and otherwise repeal the National Republican agenda. Marshall followed *Dartmouth College v. Woodward* with a decision two weeks later in the case of *Sturgis v. Crowninshield*. This was the case that protested an open-ended New York State bankruptcy law that allowed debtors to obtain easy refuge from creditors. Marshall again struck down the state statute on the grounds that the New York law violated the obligation of contracts.

Then, in 1824, Marshall struck again at the authority of the states to interfere in the operations of the market in *Gibbons v. Ogden*. In this decision, Marshall invoked the commerce clause in Article I, Section 8, of the Constitution. It's the part that reads: "Congress shall have power to regulate commerce with foreign nations and among the several states." Well, Marshall invoked this to prevent individual states from stifling market competition. Now in this particular case, *Gibbons v. Ogden*, what was at stake was the granting of a monopoly to ferry and steamboat owners on waters running through certain states. In other words, a state legislature or a state in some other form of power would grant to a particular steamboat company exclusive monopolistic rights to its waterways.

Well, Marshall argued that states like New York or by extension states bordering on the Mississippi River that share bays, lakes, and rivers with other states, states like that have to surrender their sovereignty over those shared waters and permit free competition among whatever entrepreneurs launched steamboats or other commercial vessels on them. What was Marshall doing except putting private contract rights beyond the reach of even state governments, and thus making the United States safe for the penetration of capitalist markets? That he could so with a wave of his judicial hand enraged the 76-year-old Thomas Jefferson, who had to mortgage Monticello to the hilt after the Panic of 1819 in order to pay off his creditors. "The great object of my fear is the federal judiciary," Jefferson wrote in 1819. "That body, like gravity, ever acting with noiseless foot and unalarming advance, gaining grounds step-by-step and holding what it gains, is engulfing insidiously the special governments into the jaws of that which feeds them."

There was still one last way for the old Republicans to turn the tide against the penetration of the market. They could turn from the state legislatures and the federal judiciary to the national political process. They could appeal to the new democratic majorities. They could elect a president who would restrain Congress, slay the national bank, and clean out the Supreme Court. Now, such a task would require a leader of mammoth ambition and will, yet one whose character would be saved from corruption by the love of the people and his heroism of soul. Among the Republicans there existed only one such candidate. He was the hero of New Orleans—Andrew Jackson of Tennessee.

Maps

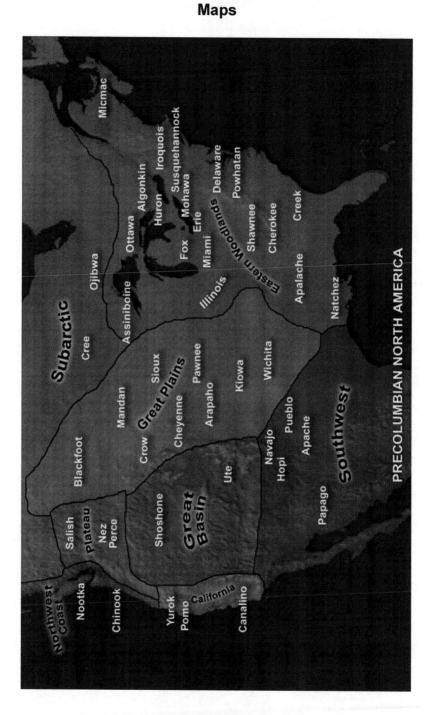

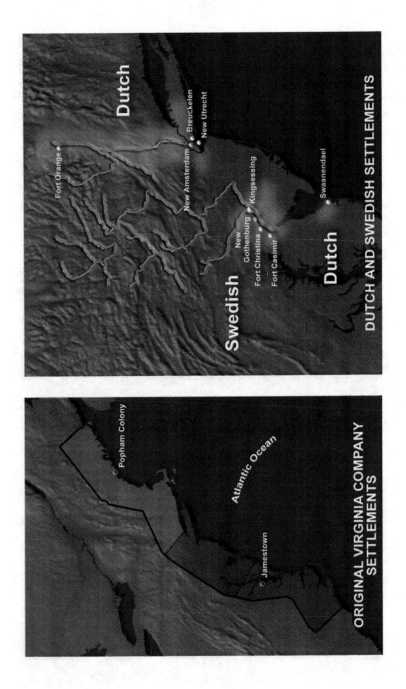

Dutch

Fort Orange

Breuckelen
New Utrecht

New Amsterdam

Kingsessing

Swedish

New
Gothenburg
Fort Christina

Fort Casimir

Swaanendael

Dutch

DUTCH AND SWEDISH SETTLEMENTS

Popham Colony

Atlantic Ocean

Jamestown

ORIGINAL VIRGINIA COMPANY
SETTLEMENTS

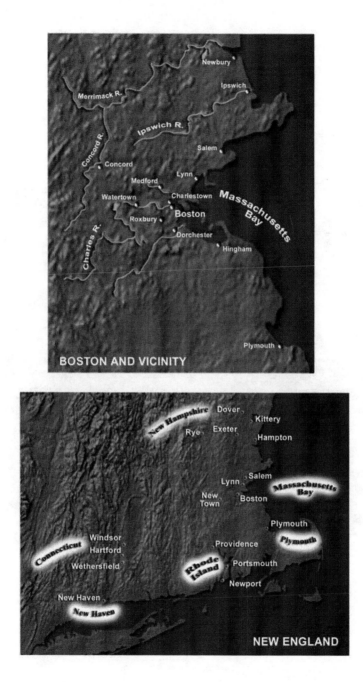

BOSTON AND VICINITY

NEW ENGLAND

SOUTHERN SETTLEMENTS

Maryland ○ St. Mary's City

○ Jamestown

Virginia

○ New Berne

Carolina

Georgia ○ Charleston

○ Beaufort

○ New Inverness

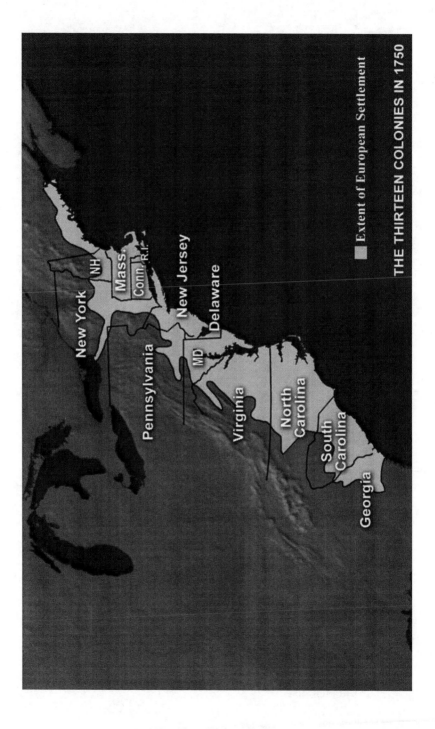

THE THIRTEEN COLONIES IN 1750

■ Extent of European Settlement

New Hampshire (NH)
Massachusetts (Mass.)
Connecticut (Conn.)
Rhode Island (R.I.)
New York
New Jersey
Delaware
Pennsylvania
Maryland (MD)
Virginia
North Carolina
South Carolina
Georgia

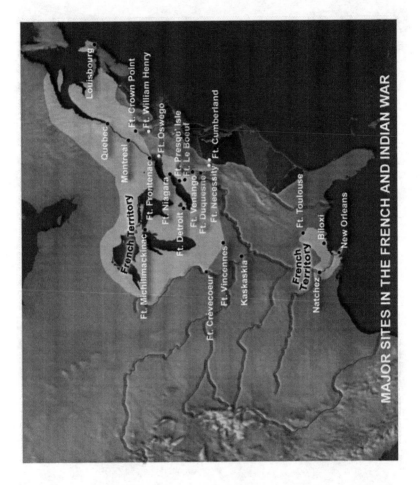

MAJOR SITES IN THE FRENCH AND INDIAN WAR

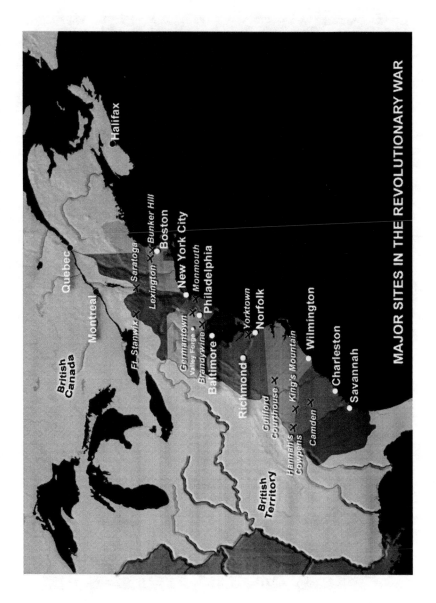

MAJOR SITES IN THE REVOLUTIONARY WAR

THE FAILED STATE OF FRANKLIN

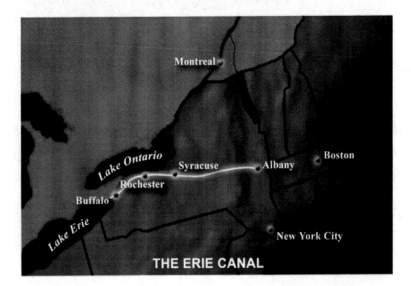

THE ERIE CANAL

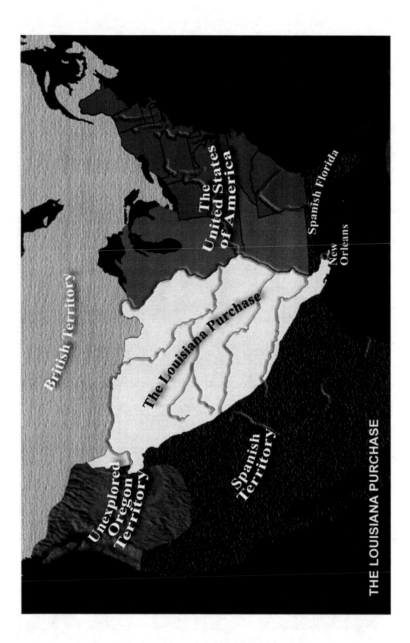

THE LOUISIANA PURCHASE

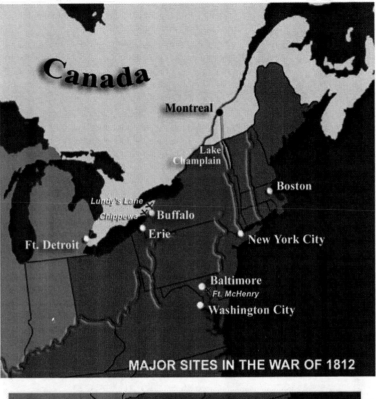

MAJOR SITES IN THE WAR OF 1812

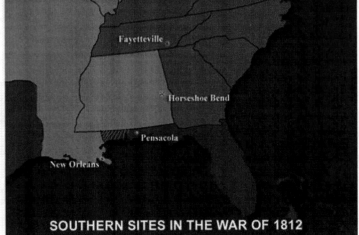

SOUTHERN SITES IN THE WAR OF 1812

©2003 The Teaching Company.

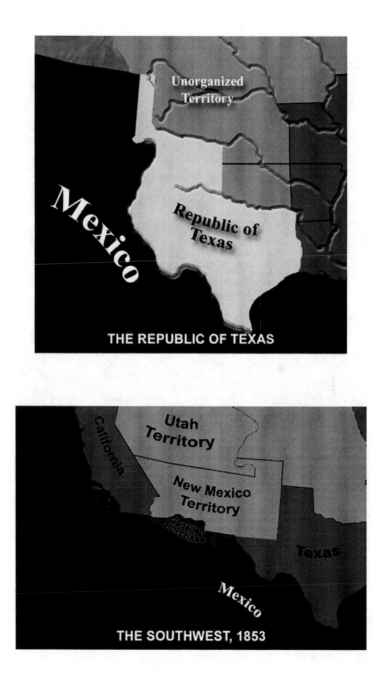

THE REPUBLIC OF TEXAS

THE SOUTHWEST, 1853

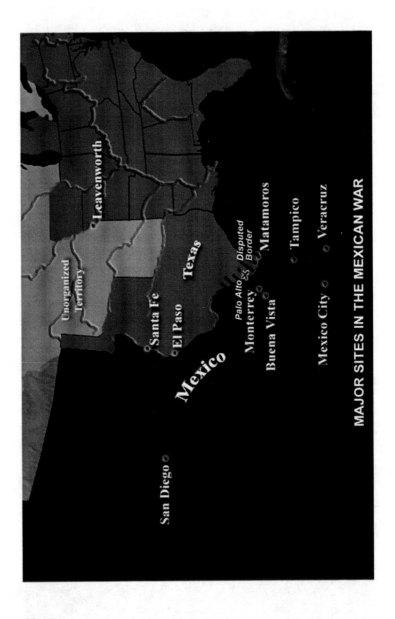

MAJOR SITES IN THE MEXICAN WAR

Timeline

Oct. 12, 1492............................Christopher Columbus makes the first modern transatlantic crossing from Europe.

Feb. 19, 1519............................Hernando Cortez sets sail from Cuba to begin the conquest of Mexico.

1585–1587.................................Sir Walter Raleigh twice is unsuccessful in planting English colonies on the Outer Banks.

May 24, 1607 ....The Virginia Company establishes an English colony on the James River at Jamestown.

Summer 1608............................Quebec established by Samuel de Champlain.

Sept. 12, 1609 ....Henry Hudson begins exploration of the Hudson River for the Dutch West Indies Company.

May–June 1626.........................Dutch purchase ground to establish a colony, New Amsterdam, on Manhattan Island.

June 17, 1630 ....Massachusetts Bay Company arrives to begin settlement at Boston.

Oct. 28, 1636............................Harvard College founded in Cambridge, Massachusetts.

Aug. 27, 1664............................Peter Stuyvesant surrenders New Amsterdam to the British, who rename it New York.

1675–1676.................................King Philip's War ravages New England.

1679–1682.................................La Salle explores the Mississippi River and claims Louisiana for France.

Aug. 10, 1680.............................Pueblo Revolt begins, destroying Spanish churches and settlements in New Mexico.

Oct. 27, 1682.............................William Penn takes possession of Pennsylvania at New Castle.

Dec. 11, 1688 ....Glorious Revolution topples King James II and replaces him with William and Mary as monarchs.

Feb. 8, 1693...............................Charter granted to found the College of William and Mary.

Nov. 8, 1739..............................George Whitefield arrives in Philadelphia as part of his first evangelical preaching tour.

July 2, 1741 ....Jonathan Edwards delivers his sermon "Sinners in the Hands of an Angry God" at Enfield, Massachusetts (now Connecticut).

May 28, 1754 ....George Washington surrenders Virginia militia at Fort Necessity, beginning the French and Indian War.

July 9, 1755...............................British troops under General Edward Braddock defeated by French and Indians near Fort Duquesne.

Sept. 18, 1759 ....British capture Quebec, and effective military resistance by the French in Canada ends.

Oct. 25, 1760.............................George III becomes king of England.

1761–1766..................................Controversy in the colonies over writs of assistance.

Feb. 10, 1763..............................Treaty of Paris signed, making Great Britain dominant in North America.

May 7–Nov. 28, 1763 ....Pontiac lays siege to Fort Detroit as part of Pontiac's Rebellion.

March 22, 1765 ....Parliament imposes the Stamp Act, then rescinds it after violent colonial protests.

July 2, 1767...............................Townsend Duties enacted.

March 5, 1770 ....The Boston Massacre leaves five dead in front of the Boston Customs House.

May 10, 1773 ....Tea Act becomes law.

Dec. 16, 1773 ....Boston Tea Party.

Sept. 5–Oct. 26, 1774................Meeting of the First Continental Congress in Philadelphia.

April 18–19, 1775 ....Battles of Lexington and Concord.

May 10, 1775 ....Second Continental Congress meets.

June 17, 1775 ....Battle of Bunker Hill.

Jan. 10, 1776 ....Thomas Paine publishes *Common Sense*.

July 4, 1776...............................Declaration of American Independence.

Dec. 18–June 9, 1777–1778.......Continental Army's winter encampment at Valley Forge, Pennsylvania.

March 1, 1780 ....Pennsylvania Act for Emancipation, first provision for gradual abolition of slavery in America.

March 1, 1781 ....Articles of Confederation ratified.

Oct. 19, 1781.............................Lord Cornwallis surrenders British forces at Yorktown.

1782 ....Hector St. John Crèvecoeur publishes *Letters from an American Farmer*.

Sept. 3, 1783 ....Treaty of Paris confirms independence of the United States from Great Britain.

May 20, 1785 ....Confederation Congress passes Land Ordinance on the organization of the western lands.

Jan. 25, 1787 ....Shay's Rebellion climaxes in an assault on the federal arsenal at Springfield, Massachusetts.

May 25–Sept. 17, 1787 ....Constitutional Convention meets in Philadelphia and draws up a new federal Constitution.

July 13, 1787.............................Confederation Congress adopts the Northwest Ordinance.

Oct.–Aug. 1787–88....................James Madison, Alexander Hamilton, and John Jay publish *The Federalist.*

April 30, 1789 ....George Washington sworn in as the first president of the United States.

Jan. 14, 1790 ....The first of Hamilton's three "reports"—the *Report on the Public Credit*—is read to Congress.

Aug. 7–Nov. 19, 1791................Whiskey Rebellion in western Pennsylvania.

Dec. 15, 1791 ....Bill of Rights ratified.

March 14, 1794 ....Eli Whitney files a patent on the cotton gin, which he had designed and built the previous year while working as a family tutor on a Georgia plantation.

Oct. 8–Nov. 8, 1797–98.............XYZ Affair outlined in dispatches from John Marshall, Timothy Pickering, and Elbridge Gerry.

Summer 1798............................June 18, 25/July 6, 14: Alien and Sedition Acts passed by Congress.

June 1, 1812 .... President Madison asks for declaration of war against Great Britain, beginning the War of 1812.

Oct. 5, 1813 .... William Henry Harrison wins a victory for the United States at the battle of the Thames.

Dec. 24, 1814 .... Treaty of Ghent ends the War of 1812.

Jan. 9, 1815 .... Andrew Jackson victorious at the battle of New Orleans.

March 14, 1816 .... Second Bank of the United States chartered by Congress.

March 20, 1816 .... Justice Joseph Story hands down Supreme Court decision in *Martin v. Hunter's Lessee.*

July 4, 1817 .... Work begins on the Erie Canal.

Feb. 2, 1819 .... *Dartmouth College v. Woodward* upholds the sanctity of contract.

Feb. 17, 1819 .... Chief Justice Marshall writes opinion for unanimous Supreme Court in *Sturgis v. Crowninshield.*

March 6, 1819 .... *McCulloch v. Maryland* establishes supremacy of federal jurisdiction over state.

Spring 1819 .... Panic of 1819 begins with fall in British commodity prices.

Feb. 16, 1820 .... Missouri Compromise adopted.

July 1822 .... Slave conspiracy under Denmark Vesey prompts panic and retribution in Charleston.

Dec. 2, 1823 .... President James Monroe's annual message to Congress articulates the Monroe Doctrine; James Fenimore Cooper begins his "Leatherstocking

Tales" with the publication of *The Pioneers*.

Jan. 14, 1824 ....Henry Clay begins exposition of the "American System" before Congress.

March 2, 1824 ....Chief Justice Marshall hands down opinion for a unanimous Supreme Court in *Gibbons v. Ogden*.

Feb. 9, 1825..............................Election of John Quincy Adams as president in the House of Representatives, after the "corrupt bargain."

March 1, 1826 ....East Chelmsford, Massachusetts, incorporated as Lowell as it becomes the most important center of textile manufacturing in the United States.

July 18–25, 1827........................New Lebanon Conference on revivalism.

July 4, 1828..............................Construction begins on Baltimore & Ohio Railroad.

Jan. 19–27, 1830 ....Webster-Hayne debates.

Jan. 1, 1831 ....William Lloyd Garrison begins publishing *The Liberator*.

Aug. 22, 1831............................Nat Turner leads a bloody slave insurrection in southeastern Virginia.

July 10, 1832.............................President Jackson vetoes re-charter of the Second Bank of the United States.

Nov. 24, 1832............................South Carolina state convention nullifies federal tariffs of 1828 and 1832.

Dec. 4, 1833 ....Founding of the American Anti-Slavery Society.

April 14, 1834 ....Henry Clay applies the term *Whig* to the anti-Jackson opposition.

March 6, 1836 ....Fall of the Alamo.

April 10, 1836 ....Charles Grandison Finney opens the Broadway Tabernacle in New York City.

Feb. 12, 1837..............................Chief Justice Roger Taney writes opinion for a narrow majority in *Charles River Bridge v. Warren Bridge*.

Aug. 31, 1837..............................Ralph Waldo Emerson delivers "The American Scholar" to the Harvard Phi Beta Kappa society.

Aug.–Dec. 1838 ....Forcible removal of 15,000 Cherokee Indians (the "Trail of Tears") begins.

Sept. 3, 1838 ....Frederick Douglass flees slavery to Philadelphia.

July 1840....................................Margaret Fuller begins publication of *The Dial*.

March 9, 1841 ....Justice Joseph Story, in *U.S. v. The Amistad*, frees slaves who rose in mutiny aboard slave ship *Amistad* in 1837.

April 4, 1841 ....President William Henry Harrison, the first Whig president, becomes the first president to die in office.

May 11–12, 1846 ....Congress approves President Polk's request for a declaration of war, beginning the Mexican War.

June 19, 1846 ....First game of baseball played on rules designed by Alexander Cartwright.

Feb. 22–23, 1847.........................Battle of Buena Vista.

Sept. 14, 1847 .... Winfield Scott captures Mexico City.

Feb. 2, 1848 .... Treaty of Guadalupe Hidalgo ends the Mexican War and provides for cession of 500,000 square miles to the United States.

July 19–20, 1848 .... Seneca Falls Convention on women's rights.

Jan. 19, 1850 .... Henry Clay introduces the bills that will make up the Compromise of 1850.

Glossary

abolitionism: A movement that gathered public visibility beginning in the 1830s; dedicated to the immediate and complete abolition of slavery in the United States.

agrarian: A term describing a cluster of ideas that located political economic virtue in agricultural employment, including independent land ownership and self-provision from the land, minimal land taxation, decentralized patterns of living, and patriarchy (in both gender and racial terms).

American System: Popularized by Henry Clay, this became the Whig economic platform and included federal government sponsorship for infrastructure ("internal improvements"), federal subsidies for manufacturing, and a fiscal system that helped fund entrepreneurship and contain the costs of risk.

Anglican: Term applied to describe the Church of England and its doctrines or to individual members of that Church; not actually used before the 19th century.

antislavery: The larger segment of opinion that opposed slavery, but not necessarily through immediate abolition.

assimilation: The process by which immigrants are brought into conformity with the dominant culture around them and in which they embrace the dominant values and reject those associated with their culture or country of origin.

business cycle: The pattern of alternating economic expansions and contractions that characterizes production and consumption in the various forms of unregulated market economies.

Calvinism: A system of religious doctrine developed by John Calvin that taught the unlimited sovereignty and power of God in ordering all human affairs and, thereby, undercut the demands for loyalty required by many governments and state-sponsored churches; its specific teachings are sometimes defined by the acronym TULIP (total depravity, unconditional election, limited atonement, irresistible grace, perseverance of the saints).

capitalism: An economic system in which (a) goods and services are sold at prices higher than their actual cost of production, with the difference between the two saved or reinvested in the production of still more goods and services; (b) resources for exchange and for initial investments in production are made available in the form of credit from financial institutions, such as banks; (c) minimal state regulation allows free movement of credit, resources, and commercial strategies; and (d) a spirit of entrepreneurship, rational abstraction, and disciplined work habits prevails.

class: A system of hierarchical social organization, based on acquired or inherited property holding and wealth and attaching various cultural attributes to each class.

colonization: In the 19th century, this term described a variety of plans proposed for repatriating freed slaves back to Africa rather than integrating them into civil and social life.

common sense philosophy: Term used to describe a system of presentational realism that asserted that the mind could directly know the objects of its ideas and, as such, could have direct and accurate intuitions of both objective reality and the moral content of objects and of internal mental processes, from which a rational and orderly system of understanding can be constructed on inductive (or Baconian) principles.

culture: The production and organization of symbols, attitudes, ideas, processes, and entertainment that express the common assumptions of a society or of groups in that society; can exist as folk, vernacular, or elite culture.

deism: General term describing a religion based on rational deduction from the evidences of nature of the existence and attributes of a supreme deity, rather than from an authoritative supernatural revelation.

democrat: Term for the political party begun as the Democratic-Republicans under Jefferson and Madison; sometimes shortened to "Republicans." In the 1820s, when a splinter group of National Republicans developed and split off to become the Whigs, the party became known simply as "Democrats" and became the vehicle for expressing the political attitudes and culture symbolized by Andrew Jackson.

electoral college: A provision in the Constitution designed to de-politicize the presidential election process by having electors in each state cast votes, based on the winner of the most votes in their states, for the president and vice president, with each state having as many votes as its combined number of senators and representatives in Congress.

Enlightenment: An intellectual movement born out of the scientific revolution of the 17th century that flourished on both sides of the Atlantic in the 18th century. The movement was characterized by confidence in reason as the means of solving practical, religious, and philosophical problems; an effort to approximate the order of nature; and a commitment to criticism as a means of discovery.

Evangelicalism: A form of Protestant Christian religious expression growing out of the Great Awakenings of the 18th century; marked by dramatic religious transformation, the location of religious authority in the Bible rather than in reason or in religious authorities, and a disposition to extend moral reform generally across society.

factory: A system in which workers trained in the production of a specific commodity or similar commodities labor for wages, produce individual parts of such commodities for assembly by other workers (rather than each worker producing the entire commodity), and use a common source of artificial power for the production process.

free labor: An economic system in which an individual, protected by natural and civil rights, is free to seek terms of employment, look for pay in the form of cash wages, and may accumulate sufficient capital through work and savings to acquire property and hire others.

frigate: A warship of the last era of wooden fighting ships, of medium size and armament (carrying anywhere from 44 to 56 cannon of varying weight), between a sloop and a ship-of-the-line.

Half-Way Covenant: A redefinition of the exacting standards of church membership originally laid down by New England Puritans, so that those children of church members who had not experienced religious conversion for themselves could nevertheless be admitted to one of the sacraments, baptism, and brought under church discipline.

indentured servant: An individual who sells rights to a term of service (usually seven years) in exchange for the costs of passage to America.

Jeffersonian: Refers to a system of ideas articulated by Thomas Jefferson, John Randolph of Roanoke, and John Taylor of Caroline that promoted agrarianism and states' rights and discouraged concentrations of fiscal and commercial power in governments, cities, institutions, and industries.

joint-stock companies: An early form of corporate organization, designed to limit risk and maximize resources by allowing individuals to contribute to a capital fund through the purchase of shares; this system limited losses to the value of shares bought and permitted sharing of profits through the payment of dividends based on the number of shares.

judicial review: The power of the federal courts to determine the legal standing and/or constitutionality of state or federal legislative actions.

jurisprudence: The theory of law; for example, a jurisprudence of "judicial restraint" would favor minimizing the intervention of judges in legislative matters.

laissez-faire: From the French, "let it be as they wish"; an economic attitude springing from Adam Smith that held that governments should exercise as small an active role as possible in a nation's economic activities and decisions.

liberalism: From the Latin *liber*, for "free"; a political and economic attitude developed at the end of the 17th century and growing to full stature in the late 18th and early 19th centuries. This view based organization of human societies on (a) the possession of natural rights rather than inherited status; (b) the notion of a "state of nature" in which the unrestrained competition for scarce resources induced people to create civil societies as a "social contract" for the purpose of acquiring and protecting property; and (c) the notion that the legitimacy of civil societies depended entirely on the securing of natural and civil rights and could be changed if it failed to do so.

Manifest Destiny: Phrase coined by Jacksonian journalist John O'Sullivan in 1845 that expressed the belief that the United States was clearly, or "manifestly," destined by divine providence, cultural superiority, or racial paternalism to extend U.S. sovereignty over the entire North American continent.

market: Originally a literal physical location but, in the 19th century, increasingly an abstract "place" in which sellers of goods and services compete with other sellers for the attention and business of consumers.

mercantilism: The view that national economies constitute resources that the state must manage in order to maximize, through regulation and subsidization, the survival of the state; especially applicable to the preservation of domestic resources and reserves of gold or silver.

militia: The civilian military forces of each state, who trained for military purposes on indifferent and occasional schedules and were available for active duty on the call of the state's governor or, in time of war or insurrection, by the president of the United States.

mobility: The concept that class, tradition, ethnicity, or religion are no barriers to economic or geographical movement.

moral philosophy: The study of practical applications of religious or philosophical teaching that formed the core of 18th- and 19th-century college curricula.

nativism: Fear of, or prejudice against, those not native born in the United States or those retaining loyalty to foreign languages, ethnic identities, or religions.

nullification: The doctrine, articulated first in the Virginia and Kentucky Resolutions, then by John Calhoun in the Nullification Crisis, that held that state governments have the power to veto, or nullify, the operation of federal laws within their bounds.

plantations: Term used to describe Britain's North American colonies from the view of the royal government. The implication was that the North American colonies were merely settlements with no forms of self-government that the crown was obligated to consult.

public lands: The vast holdings owned by the federal government in the areas ceded to the United States by the Treaty of Paris or acquired by the Louisiana Purchase or the Mexican Cession and whose sales were a major source of revenue for the federal government.

Puritanism: A religious protest movement in English Protestantism that identified itself doctrinally with Calvinism, set extremely high moral standards for admission to church membership, and insisted on disentangling the church from state control, even to the point of authorizing individual congregations to manage their own affairs (Congregationalism).

racism: A belief that certain physical marks categorize people into races and that these can be ranked hierarchically in moral, intellectual, or physical terms that permit members of a "superior" race to stigmatize, oppress, or exploit members of an "inferior" race.

Republicanism: Any form of political organization or ideology that (a) repudiates monarchy, oligarchy, or tyranny; (b) replaces government by self-interest and patronage with public spirit and considerations of merit; (c) lodges political authority in the community as a whole while restricting legislative, judicial, or executive responsibilities in the state to those enjoying popular endorsement; and (d) may be more or less democratic in the identification of those who are accorded civil rights, especially the vote. Sometimes distinguished into "classical" republicanism, which stresses public spirit and community, and "liberal" republicanism, which legitimates the pursuit of economic and political self-interest as leading to the greatest good.

Romanticism: A reaction to the rationalism of the Enlightenment that valued community with nature; the power of emotion, passion, or sentiment over reason; a belief that "organic" and nonrational factors governed human behavior; and an individual subjectivity.

sedition: Treason, as in the Alien and Sedition Acts.

specie: Hard coin, in gold or silver, as opposed to paper money, stock certificates, or credit.

states' rights: A political doctrine rooted in the view that the states of the Union are its primary political units and have surrendered only limited aspects of sovereignty to the federal government.

suffrage: The civil right to vote.

tariffs: A tax laid on imported goods to be paid by the importer, often levied as a way of adding to the costs of foreign-produced goods in order to give competitive advantage to domestically produced goods.

temperance: A reform movement beginning in the 1820s that sought to restrict the consumption of hard alcoholic spirits through moral exhortation; eventually, the movement became interchangeable with the idea of total abstinence from all fermented liquors and political movements to ban alcohol production and distribution.

transcendentalism: Describes the beliefs of a group of New England Romantic philosophers who sought to "transcend" the Realist epistemology of the dominant "common sense" philosophy by discovering ideas of moral truth and beauty apart from sensation. The transcendentalists espoused reform movements based on communities that identified norms for behavior through mystical delight in nature and the discovery of "authenticity."

Unitarianism: A religious movement in 18th- and 19th-century New England Congregationalism that rejected the traditional tenets of Calvinism, in particular, the notion that God existed as three persons in a Trinity (composed of God the Father, Jesus Christ the Son, and the Holy Spirit), in favor of a "rational" reading of the Bible that found only one "person" in God and, therefore, redefined Jesus Christ as a being of a separate and lower order.

Utopianism: From Thomas More's *Utopia* (as derived from the Greek, *eutopia*, or "good place"), the quest for a perfectly ordered society in which inequality, crime, poverty, and suffering have been abolished by a readjustment of social relations, either through rational management or strict adherence to religious revelation.

veto: From the Latin for "I prevent," the term is used in article 1, section 9, of the Constitution to describe the power of the president to prevent Congressional legislation from passing into law.

voluntary societies: Describes self-organized associations of citizens for specific goals, usually religious, moral, or philanthropic, that the federal government was restricted by the Constitution from publicly pursuing or was given no mandate to pursue.

Whig: Originally, in English political history, the "country" party, opposed to the "court" party and absolute monarchy, this became the name of a party described in 1834 by Henry Clay as the new opposition to "King" Andrew Jackson and the Democrats.

Biographical Notes

John Adams (1735–1826). American lawyer, member of the Continental Congress, and second president of the United States. Moving force for American independence in the Revolution and major figure in the Federalist Party.

John Quincy Adams (1767–1848). American lawyer and sixth president of the United States. Elected president by the House of Representatives in the contested election of 1824 but tainted by suspicion of a "corrupt bargain" struck with Henry Clay.

Nicholas Biddle (1786–1844). American financier. President of the Second Bank of the United States, who triggered the "Bank War" of 1832 by applying for re-chartering of the bank in the face of Andrew Jackson's opposition.

John Burgoyne (1722–1792). British playwright, politician, and general. Commanded British invasion force from Canada in 1777, only to be defeated and forced to surrender his army at Saratoga, New York.

Aaron Burr (1756–1836). American lawyer and vice president of the United States. Allied himself with Thomas Jefferson and served as Jefferson's first vice president but alienated many Jeffersonians and was dropped from the ticket in 1804. Notorious for having killed Alexander Hamilton in a duel in 1804. Indicted for treason in 1807 after a plot to set up a separate republic in the southwest.

Horace Bushnell (1802–1876). American Congregational theologian. Proposed new ways of understanding traditional Calvinist religious language.

John Caldwell Calhoun (1782–1850). American politician and vice president of the United States. Attempted to shield the South from nationalist economic schemes; Calhoun proposed "nullification" of federal tariffs as a state's right and later demanded the opening of the Mexican Cession to slavery.

Henry Clay (1777–1852). American politician and secretary of state. Originally one of the "hawks" who agitated for the War of 1812, he became the author of the "American System" and founder of the Whig Party.

DeWitt Clinton (1769–1828). American politician and governor of New York. Proposed construction of the Erie Canal in 1816.

James Fenimore Cooper (1789–1851). American novelist. Introduced Romanticism to American literature through his series of "Leatherstocking Tales" (1823–1841), including *The Last of the Mohicans* (1826).

Charles Cornwallis (First Marquis and second Earl Cornwallis, 1738–1805). British general. Served in the Seven Years' War and the Revolution, in which he commanded the major British field force in the American South. Forced to surrender at Yorktown, Virginia, in 1781.

John Dickinson (1732–1808). American lawyer and politician. Served in the Continental Congress and was largely responsible for drafting the Articles of Confederation. Chaired the Annapolis Convention in 1786 and wrote on behalf of the new federal Constitution.

Jonathan Edwards (1703–1758). American Congregational theologian. Pastor of Northampton, Massachusetts, during the Great Awakening and author of important treatises defending the awakening and traditional Puritan Calvinism.

Ralph Waldo Emerson (1803–1882). American essayist and philosopher. Originally a Unitarian minister, he became the leading light of transcendentalism and popularized Romanticism in American philosophy.

Charles Grandison Finney (1792–1875). American Presbyterian theologian and educator. The most famous preacher of the Second Great Awakening, he helped found Oberlin College and served as pastor of Oberlin's First Church.

Benjamin Franklin (1706–1790). American printer, publisher, politician, scientist, and diplomat. Served in the Second Continental Congress and helped negotiate the Treaty of Paris. Signed both the Declaration of Independence and the Constitution.

Robert Fulton (1765–1815). American inventor. Designed and built the first commercially successful steamboat, the *Clermont*.

Thomas Gage (1720–1787). British general. Commanded British forced in North America from 1763 to 1775. Organized the raid that became the battles of Lexington and Concord.

William Lloyd Garrison (1805–1879). American newspaper editor and abolitionist. Founded the abolitionist newspaper *The Liberator* in 1831 and founded the American Anti-Slavery Society.

Alexander Hamilton (1757–1804). American lawyer, soldier, and first secretary of the treasury. His three Reports to Congress as treasury secretary helped shape the economic development of the American Republic.

William Henry Harrison (1773–1841). American soldier, politician, and eighth president of the United States. Cleared the Northwest Territory of Indian resistance at the battle of Tippecanoe in 1811 and defeated the British at the battle of the Thames in 1813 during the War of 1812. The first Whig president and the first president to die in office.

Nathaniel Hawthorne (1804–1864). American novelist. Originally influenced by transcendentalism, he turned to crafting an outstanding series of historical novels, especially *The Scarlet Letter* (1850) and *The House of Seven Gables* (1851).

Charles Hodge (1797–1878). American Presbyterian theologian. As seminary professor at Princeton Theological Seminary, he was the principal figure in the creation of the Princeton Theology.

Sir William Howe (1729–1814). British general. Commanded British forces in North America from 1775 to 1778, winning a series of victories over the Continental Army at Long Island, Brandywine, and Germantown, but he was unsuccessful in completely snuffing out the Revolution.

Henry Hudson (d. 1611). British navigator and explorer. Sponsored by the Dutch West Indies Company, he discovered the Hudson River in 1609 but died in a futile attempt to discover a northwest passage to China.

Andrew Jackson (1767–1845). American soldier and seventh president of the United States. Lionized for his victory over the British at New Orleans in 1815, Jackson was denied the presidency through the "corrupt bargain" of 1824 but was elected in 1828 and 1832 and pursued aggressive policies against the Second Bank of the

United States, the Cherokee Indians, and southern threats of nullification of federal legislation.

Thomas Jefferson (1743–1826). American lawyer, author, first secretary of state, and third president of the United States. Author of the Declaration of Independence and enemy of the Federalists, he was the architect of the Democratic-Republican Party's agrarian ideology.

Marie Joseph Paul Yves Roch Gilbert du Motier, Marquis de Lafayette (1757–1834). French nobleman who volunteered his services as an aide to George Washington during the Revolution.

Robert Cavelier, Sieur de La Salle (1643–1687). French explorer. Explored the Great Lakes and Mississippi River valley for France and died trying to establish a settlement at the mouth of the Mississippi in 1687.

Ann Lee (1736–1784). English religious mystic. Founder of the communitarian sect known as the "Shakers" in 1774.

Meriwether Lewis (1774–1809). American soldier and explorer. Together with William Clark, he was commissioned by Thomas Jefferson to survey the Louisiana Purchase and carried out Jefferson's directive with a Corps of Discovery from 1804 to 1806, having reached the Pacific Ocean and returned with the loss of only one member of the expedition.

Francis Cabot Lowell (1775–1817). American industrialist. Founded the Boston Manufacturing Company and created the first large-scale textile mills in America at Waltham, Massachusetts.

James Madison (1751–1836). American lawyer, secretary of state, and fourth president of the United States. Joined with Hamilton and John Jay to argue for ratification of the Constitution by writing *The Federalist Papers* but supported Jefferson in the political conflict with federalism. Presided over American involvement in the War of 1812.

Horace Mann (1796–1859). American lawyer and educator. Designed a comprehensive renovation of the Massachusetts public education system and created the outline of the modern public school system.

John Marshall (1755–1835). American lawyer and chief justice of the U.S. Supreme Court. A Federalist appointed by John Adams to the Supreme Court, his long tenure as chief justice allowed Marshall to establish important principles of judicial review, the supremacy of federal over state authority, and the protection of the manufacturing economy.

Cotton Mather (1663–1728). American Congregational clergyman. Tireless promoter of schemes for public welfare and the reconciliation of Calvinism with the New Philosophy.

James Monroe (1758–1831). American diplomat and fifth president of the United States.

William Paterson (1745–1806). American lawyer and politician, born in Ireland. Architect of the "New Jersey Plan" at the Constitutional Convention in 1787.

Charles Cotesworth Pinckney (1746–1825) American lawyer, judge, diplomat, and politician. One of three American diplomats sent by President Adams to negotiate with the French Directory, only to be confronted by demands for bribes in the XYZ Affair.

Pontiac (1720–1769). Ottawa chieftain. Organized an intertribal offensive against the British at the close of the French and Indian War.

Paul Revere (1735–1818). Boston artisan. Carried warning of British raid to Lexington on the night of April 18–19, 1775.

Winfield Scott (1786–1866). American soldier. Commanded the principal American field force in the Mexican War, winning successive victories in 1847 that culminated in the capture of Mexico City.

Elizabeth Cady Stanton (1815–1902). American feminist. A pioneer of awarding civil equality to women, she organized the first women's rights convention at Seneca Falls, New York, in 1848.

Friedrich Wilhelm Ludolf Gerhard Augustin von Steuben (1730–1794). Prussian mercenary. Hired in 1777 to train the Continental Army at its winter encampment in Valley Forge, Pennsylvania.

Tecumseh (1768–1813). Shawnee chieftain. Organized a coalition of Indian tribes to resist white expansion in the Northwest Territory. After his forces were defeated at Tippecanoe by William Henry

Harrison, he fled to Canada and fought with the British in the War of 1812. He was killed at the battle of the Thames.

George Washington (1732–1799). first president of the United States. Commanded the Continental Army in the Revolution, presided over the Constitutional Convention, and became a leading figure of the Federalists.

Daniel Webster (1782–1852). American lawyer and politician. Involved in the major cases of the Marshall Court, including *Gibbons v. Ogden, McCulloch vs. Maryland,* and *Dartmouth College vs. Woodward*. The greatest orator in the Senate, he attacked nullification and disunion in his great Second Reply to Hayne (1830).

Eli Whitney (1765–1825). American inventor. Inventor of the cotton gin, which made the commercial growth of cotton feasible, and the manufacturing system of interchangeable parts.

John Winthrop (1588–1649). English lawyer and Puritan, first governor of Massachusetts Bay. Led the Puritan exodus to New England in 1630 and founded the town of Boston.

John Witherspoon (1723–1794). American Presbyterian clergyman and president of Princeton College, born in Scotland. Became president of Princeton in 1768 and served in the Continental Congress. Advocate of Scottish "common sense" philosophy and the necessity of public religion to ensure virtue in a republic.

Bibliography

Essential Reading

Bailyn, Bernard. *The Ideological Origins of the American Revolution*. Cambridge, MA: Harvard University Press, 1967. A path-breaking work that reoriented our understanding of the political ideas of the American revolutionaries and their roots in five major sources of Whig thinking.

Boorstin, Daniel. *The Lost World of Thomas Jefferson*. New York: Henry Holt, 1948. An "intellectual biography" of the mind and ideas of Thomas Jefferson.

Butler, Jon. *Awash in a Sea of Faith: Christianizing the American People*. Cambridge, MA: Harvard University Press, 1990. Argues that religion established a comparatively feeble presence in early America, despite the presence of radical religious groups, such as the Puritans and Quakers, but eventually, through its own energies, succeeded in rising to cultural prominence in the early republic.

Carey, George W., and James McClellan. *The Federalist*. Indianapolis, IN: Liberty Fund, 2001. The best collection of the famous articles by Hamilton, Jay, and Madison advocating ratification of the federal Constitution, with the text of the Constitution keyed to all relevant sections of *The Federalist*.

Clark, Christopher. *The Roots of Rural Capitalism: Western Massachusetts, 1780–1861*. Ithaca, NY: Cornell University Press, 1990. A thorough and eye-opening investigation of the opening of rural western Massachusetts to commercial market agriculture, with its attendant social dislocations.

Elkins, Stanley, and Eric McKitrick. *The Age of Federalism: The Early American Republic, 1788–1800*. New York: Oxford University Press, 1993. The finest single-volume political history of the federal era.

Fogel, Robert William. *Without Consent or Contract: The Rise and Fall of American Slavery*. New York: W.W. Norton, 1989. The best survey of the economic nature of slavery, which Fogel argues developed into a dangerously profitable labor system before the Civil War.

Gipson, Lawrence Henry. *The British Empire before the American Revolution*. New York: Knopf, 1958–1968. A massive survey of

Britain's North American colonies and their place in the larger scheme of the British Empire, from 1748–1776, in 14 volumes.

Holt, Michael F. *The Rise and Fall of the American Whig Party: Jacksonian Politics and the Onset of the Civil War*. New York: Oxford University Press, 1999. An enormous, highly detailed history of the fortunes of the Whig Party, with particular attention to its organization for elections and its successes and failures on the state and local levels.

Howe, Daniel Walker. *The Political Culture of the American Whigs*. Chicago: University of Chicago Press, 1979. Classic explanation of the values and attitudes that stood behind the public policies of the Whigs, with separate chapters on the major Whig leaders.

Kolchin, Peter. *American Slavery, 1619–1877*. New York: Hill and Wang, 1993. A thorough survey of the social, economic, and racial aspects of southern slavery.

McCusker, John J., and Russell R. Menard. *The Economy of British America, 1607–1789*. Chapel Hill, NC: University of North Carolina Press, 1985. The standard work on the nature of the various colonial economies of British North America.

Miller, Perry. *The New England Mind: The 17th Century*. Cambridge, MA: Harvard University Press, 1939. One of the greatest pieces of American historical writing, this volume (the first of three) is an "intellectual history" of the Puritanism carried to New England in the 1600s, written around the issues of reason, scholasticism, rhetoric, and covenant theology.

Morgan, Edmund S. *American Slavery-American Freedom: The Ordeal of Colonial Virginia*. New York: W.W. Norton, 1975. A meticulous history of the settlement of Virginia, from Jamestown through Bacon's Rebellion, showing how the demand for labor shaped the movement toward slavery and how slavery, in turn, shaped the notions of freedom brought to the Revolution by the Virginia elite.

Morison, Samuel Eliot. *The European Discovery of America: The Northern Voyages, A.D. 500–1600*. New York: Oxford University Press, 1971. A narrative history of the voyages of discovery to the North American continent before the beginning of permanent English settlements.

———. *The European Discovery of America: The Southern Voyages, A.D. 1492–1616*. New York: Oxford University Press,

1974. A sequel to the previous volume, tracing the voyages, beginning with that of Columbus, that explored the Caribbean, Gulf of Mexico, and Pacific coast.

Sellers, Charles G. *The Market Revolution: Jacksonian America, 1815–1846*. New York: Oxford University Press, 1991. A highly influential survey of the era, arguing forthrightly for the importance of the penetration of capitalist markets into American life as the chief issue in American politics and culture.

Smith, Billy G. *The "Lower Sort": Philadelphia's Laboring People, 1750–1800*. Ithaca, NY: Cornell University Press, 1990. A classic social history of the working class of Philadelphia in the early republic, analyzing the city's economy, wealth-holding patterns, and the family and working lives of the poor, but without illusions about a pre-industrial "golden age."

Tocqueville, Alexis de. *Democracy in America*. Harvey C. Mansfield and Delba Winthrop, eds. Chicago: University of Chicago Press, 2000. The authoritative translation of Tocqueville's massive commentary on the nature of American democracy.

Wood, Gordon S. *The Creation of the American Republic, 1776–1789*. Chapel Hill, NC: University of North Carolina Press, 1967. Depicts the creation of an independent American Republic as the product of a violent and complex crosscurrent of conflicting ideas of liberty in the colonies and new states, rather than a single, straightforward notion of liberty.

———. *The Radicalism of the American Revolution*. New York: Knopf, 1992. Argues that American republicanism was founded on aristocratic values that the Revolution undermined, leading to the swift development of a democratic, rather than a republican, political consciousness.

Supplementary Reading

Note: Some of the following books may be out of print. Internet sites such as www.abebooks.com and www.amazon.com may be helpful in locating copies.

Alden, John Richard. *George Washington: A Biography*. Baton Rouge, LA: Louisiana State University Press, 1984. An excellent one-volume survey of Washington's life.

Appleby, Joyce. *Capitalism and a New Social Order: The Republican Vision of the 1790s*. New York: New York University

Press, 1984. Appleby argues that the republican ideology always had a strong bias toward liberal capitalism rather than toward non-market forms of "classical" republicanism.

———. *Inheriting the Revolution: The First Generation of Americans*. Cambridge, MA: Harvard University Press, 2000. A group biography of a cross-section of Americans between 1776 and 1826.

Ashworth, John. *Slavery, Capitalism, and Politics in the Antebellum Republic*. Cambridge: Cambridge University Press, 1996. A lengthy examination of the economic presuppositions of Whig and Democratic political thought.

Baker, Jean H. *Affairs of Party: The Political Culture of Northern Democrats in the Mid-nineteenth Century*. Ithaca, NY: Cornell University Press, 1983. An outstanding survey of the attitudes that formed Democratic "political culture" and underlay explicit Democratic policies.

Banner, James M. *To the Hartford Convention: The Federalists and the Origins of Party Politics in the Early Republic, 1789–1815*. New York: Knopf, 1967. Analyzes the rise and decline of New England federalism up to the party's collapse after the Hartford Convention.

Banning, Lance. *The Jeffersonian Persuasion: Evolution of a Party Ideology*. Ithaca, NY: Cornell University Press, 1978. Explains the components and details of Jeffersonian politics and policies.

———. *The Sacred Fire of Liberty: James Madison and the Founding of the Federal Republic*. Ithaca, NY: Cornell University Press, 1995. An in-depth analysis of James Madison that sees Madison as a consistent Jeffersonian throughout his career.

Bartlett, Irving H. *Daniel Webster*. New York: W.W. Norton, 1973. A biography of Webster emphasizing the contradictions within the man and his image.

Benson, Lee. *The Concept of Jacksonian Democracy: New York as Test Case*. Princeton: Princeton University Press, 1961. A classic work asserting that Jacksonian politics was organized less around ideas and policies and more by ethnic and religious group identities.

Brooke, John L. *The Refiner's Fire: The Making of Mormon Cosmology, 1644–1844*. New York: Cambridge University Press, 1994. Fascinating tour through the world of early American mystical and cultic beliefs that eventually formed the core of Mormonism.

Brown, Thomas. *Politics and Statesmanship: Essays on the American Whig Party*. New York: Columbia University Press, 1985. Essays on Whig Party attitudes and Whig leaders.

Bushman, Richard L. *The Refinement of America: Persons, Houses, Cities*. New York: Vintage, 1992. Studies the emergence of rules and handbooks on fashion, decoration, appearances, and self-presentation in the early republic.

Carwardine, Richard J. *Evangelicals and Politics in Antebellum America*. New Haven: Yale University Press, 1993. Strongly detailed picture of the issues that bound Protestant evangelicals to the Whigs and, later, to the Republicans.

Cochran, Thomas Childs. *Frontiers of Change: Early Industrialism in America*. New York: Oxford University Press, 1981. The standard introduction and survey of the beginnings of American industrialization.

Conkin, Paul K. *The Uneasy Center: Reformed Christianity in Antebellum America*. Chapel Hill, NC: University of North Carolina Press, 1995. Discusses the major ideas and thinkers among American Calvinists in the early republic, including Nathaniel William Taylor, Charles Hodge, and John Williamson Nevin.

Conway, Thomas. *The War of American Independence, 1775–1783*. London: Edward Arnold, 1995. The American Revolution from a delightfully literate English historian's perspective, measuring the worldwide scope and impact of the Revolution.

Countryman, Edward. *The American Revolution*. New York: Hill and Wang, 1985. A social history of the American Revolution.

Cronon, William. *Changes in the Land: Indians, Colonists, and the Ecology of New England*. New York: Hill and Wang, 1983. An innovative history of the impact of European settlement on the ecology and native societies of New England, full of many surprises about both the agents and recipients of those changes.

Cross, Whitney R. *The Burned-over District: The Social and Intellectual History of Enthusiastic Religion in Western New York, 1800–1850*. Ithaca, NY: Cornell University Press, 1950. A social history of western New York and the causes and impact of the revivals and religious cults that swept through it.

Dawidoff, Robert. *The Education of John Randolph*. New York: W.W. Norton, 1979. A raffish but sympathetic biography of the savagely articulate Jeffersonian.

Demos, John Putnam. *Entertaining Satan: Witchcraft and the Culture of Early New England*. New York: Oxford University Press, 1982. A history of witchcraft in the larger context of 17th-century American culture, along with a detailed analysis of the 1692 panic in Salem, Massachusetts; the individuals who fostered it; and those who were its victims.

Douglas, Ann. *The Feminization of American Culture*. New York: Knopf, 1977. A pioneering cultural history of pre-Civil War America, with emphasis on how religion and literature came to be "feminized," or seen as primarily the sphere of women.

Dwight, Timothy. *Travels in New England and New York*. Barbara Miller Solomon, ed. Cambridge, MA: Harvard University Press, 1969. Dwight, the grandson of Jonathan Edwards, embarked on a tour of New England in 1821–1822 to capture oral histories and impressions of the region as the last colonial generation was fading from the scene.

Eisenhower, John S. D. *So Far from God: The U.S. War with Mexico, 1846–1848*. New York: Random House, 1989. The best and most thorough modern narrative of the Mexican War.

Ellis, Joseph J. *American Sphinx: The Character of Thomas Jefferson*. New York: Knopf, 1997. An analysis of the character of Jefferson, who is portrayed as a collection of ideas whose parts did not all communicate with each other.

———. *Founding Brothers: The Revolutionary Generation*. New York: Knopf, 2000.

Faragher, John Mack. *Sugar Creek: Life on the Illinois Prairie*. New Haven: Yale University Press, 1986. Focuses on the transformation of a village in central Illinois from its prairie condition to the arrival of white agricultural pioneers and, eventually, the coming of the transportation revolution and commercial agriculture.

Fiering, Norman. *Moral Philosophy at 17th-Century Harvard*. Chapel Hill: University of North Carolina Press, 1981. An important description of how the curriculum of Harvard College witnessed the replacement of Christian scholasticism with a naturalistic moral philosophy, with particular attention to the principal textbooks and the development of a distinctive psychology.

Finney, Charles Grandison. *The Memoirs of Charles G. Finney: The Complete Restored Text*. Garth M. Rosell and Richard A. G. Dupuis, eds. Grand Rapids, MI: Academie Books, 1989. A superb edition of

Finney's autobiography, with a reconstructed text and elaborate notes and identifications.

Fischer, David Hackett. *Paul Revere's Ride*. New York: Oxford University Press, 1994. Story of the first conflict of the Revolution, with the twin figures of Thomas Gage and Paul Revere at the forefront.

Flexner, James Thomas. *George Washington and the New Nation, 1783–1793*. Boston: Little, Brown, 1970. This is the third volume in the best multivolume survey of Washington's life.

———.*George Washington: Anguish and Farewell, 1793–1799*. Boston: Little, Brown,1972.

———.*George Washington in the American Revolution, 1775–1783*. Boston: Little, Brown, 1968.

———. *George Washington: The Forge of Experience, 1732–1775*. Boston: Little, Brown, 1965.

Flower, Elizabeth, and Murray G. Murphey. *A History of Philosophy in America*. New York: G.P. Putnam's Sons, 1977. The first volume of this two-volume survey of American philosophy offers an invaluable overview of the main currents of American philosophical thought from the Puritans through transcendentalism.

Frederickson, George M. *The Black Image in the White Mind: The Debate on Afro-American Character and Destiny, 1817–1914*. New York: Harper & Row, 1971. Investigates the emergence of racism and racist justifications for the social marginalization and alienation of blacks, both free and slave.

Freehling, William W. *Prelude to Civil War: The Nullification Controversy in South Carolina*. New York: Harper & Row, 1966. Standard account of the controversy between Calhoun and South Carolina, and President Andrew Jackson, over the attempted nullification of the federal tariff.

———. *The Road to Disunion*, vol. 1: *Secessionists at Bay*. New York: Oxford University Press, 1990. A large-scale study of the slave South and its internal differences over slavery.

Genovese, Eugene D. *The Political Economy of Slavery: Studies in the Economy and Society of the Slave South*. New York: Pantheon, 1965. Analyzes the connections between slaveholding and pro-slavery ideology and market capitalism.

—————. *Roll, Jordan, Roll: The World the Slaves Made*. New York: Pantheon, 1972. An intriguing interpretation of southern slavery as a pre-modern, pre-capitalist society in which slaves seized control of much of the dynamic of authority in their lives and compelled slaveowners to treat with them as workers rather than chattels.

Green, James A. *William Henry Harrison: His Life and Times*. Richmond, VA: Garrett and Massie, 1941. The principal modern biography of the first Whig president and the first president to die in office.

Greene, Jack P. *Pursuits of Happiness: The Social Development of Early Modern British Colonies and the Formation of American Culture*. Chapel Hill, NC: University of North Carolina Press, 1988. Focuses on the Chesapeake, rather than New England, as the settlement that most determined the development of American culture and offers a three-part formula of simplification, elaboration, and replication as an alternative to the New England preoccupation with "declension" as a way of understanding cultural change.

Gutman, Herbert. *The Black Family in Slavery and Freedom, 1750–1925*. New York: Pantheon, 1976. Pioneering study arguing that enslaved blacks successfully maintained family structures under the pressure of slavery and that the modern disintegration of the black family was a recent political phenomenon.

Hall, David D. *Worlds of Wonder, Days of Judgment: Popular Religious Belief in Early New England*. New York: Knopf, 1989. An innovative look into the practical beliefs and non-beliefs of New England Puritans, as opposed to an intellectual history of the clergy, concluding that the gap between the two was not nearly as wide as might be supposed.

Hambrick-Stowe, Charles E. *The Practice of Piety: Puritan Devotional Disciplines in Seventeenth-Century New England*. Chapel Hill, NC: University of North Carolina Press, 1982. A sympathetic and in-depth examination of Puritan spiritual disciplines and devotional reading.

Hamilton, Holman. *Prologue to Conflict: The Crisis and Compromise of 1850*. New York: W.W. Norton, 1964. The standard account of the political conflict over the extension of slavery into the Mexican Cession and its resolution in the Great Compromise.

Hatch, Nathan O. *The Democratization of American Christianity*. New Haven: Yale University Press, 1989. Argues that evangelical

Protestants were influenced by democratization in church structure, leadership, and theology but also contributed tremendously to it, as well.

Hickey, Donald. *The War of 1812: A Forgotten Conflict*. Urbana, IL: University of Illinois Press, 1989. A dependable narrative of the Anglo-American conflict of 1812–1815.

Hodges, Graham Russell. *Slavery and Freedom in the Rural North: African-Americans in Monmouth County, New Jersey, 1665–1865*. Madison, WI: Madison House, 1997. Studies the lives of slave and free African Americans in a central New Jersey county.

Horgan, Paul. *Conquistadors in North American History*. New York: Farrar, Straus, 1963. A delightfully written and short survey of the Spanish colonial empire in northern Mexico.

Howe, Daniel Walker. *Making the American Self: From Jonathan Edwards to Abraham Lincoln*. Cambridge, MA: Harvard University Press, 1997. Examines the creation of an American model personality, based on notions of self-control and self-transformation, which played large roles in the formation of the Whig and evangelical Protestant minds.

———. *The Unitarian Conscience: Harvard Moral Philosophy, 1805–1861*. Cambridge, MA: Harvard University Press, 1970. An engaging examination of Unitarianism's capture of Harvard and its major personalities and ethical teachings.

Isaac, Rhys. *The Transformation of Virginia, 1740–1790*. Chapel Hill, NC: University of North Carolina Press, 1982. Explores the way in which radical evangelicalism in Virginia undermined the authority of traditional Virginia elites in the 18th century and prepared Virginians for participation in the Revolution.

Jennings, Francis. *The Invasion of America: Indians, Colonialism, and the Cant of Conquest*. New York: W.W. Norton, 1975. A radical view of American colonial history that treats the process of settlement as destructive, murderous, and ruthless.

Johnson, Paul E. *A Shopkeeper's Millennium: Society and Revival in Rochester, New York, 1815–1837*. New York: Hill & Wang, 1978. Argues for a causal relationship between economic changes brought by the transportation revolution to western New York and the release from social anxiety brought by the Second Great Awakening.

Kammen, Michael. *Colonial New York: A History*. New York: Scribner, 1975. A thorough survey of New York history from the Dutch founding to the first state constitution in 1777.

Kelley, Joseph J. *Pennsylvania: The Colonial Years, 1681–1776*. A lengthy but well-written narrative of colonial Pennsylvania from William Penn to Washington's crossing of the Delaware.

Ketchum, Richard M. *Saratoga: Turning Point of America's Revolutionary War*. New York: Henry Holt, 1997. Popular account of the Revolution's most important battle.

Kramnick, Isaac. *Republicanism and Bourgeois Radicalism: Political Ideology in Late Eighteenth-Century England and America*. Ithaca, NY: Cornell University Press, 1990. The development and radicalization of middle-class Whig Republicans in the 18th-century on both sides of the Atlantic.

————, and R. Laurence Moore. *The Godless Constitution: The Case against Religious Correctness*. New York, NY : W.W. Norton & Company, 1996. A controversial and spirited argument against the notion that Christianity was ever intended by the Founders to have a public role in American political life.

Kupperman, Karen Ordahl. *Roanoke: The Abandoned Colony*. Savage, MD: Rowman and Littlefield, 1984. An intriguing and thorough history of the ill-fated Roanoke colonies.

Lambert, Frank. *Inventing the "Great Awakening."* Princeton, NJ: Princeton University Press, 1999. A cultural analysis of the way the religious revivals of the 1740s were depicted, interpreted, and reproduced.

Lebsock, Suzanne. *The Free Women of Petersburg: Status and Culture in a Southern Town, 1784–1860*. New York: W.W. Norton, 1984. Uses Petersburg, Virginia, women as models for understanding the economic and social lives of women and the numerous ways in which they carved out pockets of independence while still suffering legal disabilities.

Lepore, Jill. *The Name of War: King Philip's War and the Origins of American Identity*. New York: Knopf, 1998. A cultural history of the devastating Indian war of 1675–1676 in New England.

Lockridge, Kenneth. *A New England Town: The First Hundred Years*. New York: W.W. Norton, 1970. A social history of Dedham, Massachusetts, from its founding in 1635 as a "closed, corporate

Christian community" to its social fracturing under the stresses of demography and economics.

Lord, Walter. *The Dawn's Early Light*. New York: W.W. Norton, 1972. A popular history of the British attack on Fort McHenry in Baltimore Harbor, which not only failed to seize the fort and city, but helped produce the national anthem.

———. *A Time To Stand*. New York: Harper, 1961. A fast-paced, popular history of the fall of the Alamo, but with careful attention to a full reading of original sources.

Maier, Pauline. *American Scripture: Making the Declaration of Independence*. New York: Knopf, 1997. A vivid analysis of the sources Jefferson used in constructing the Declaration of Independence and the Declaration's subsequent standing in American history.

———. *From Resistance to Revolution: Colonial Radicals and the Development of American Opposition to Britain, 1765–1776*. New York: Vintage Books, 1972. Surveys the movement of American opposition from the Stamp Act to independence.

May, Henry F. *The Enlightenment in America*. New York: Oxford University Press, 1976. An enormously literate and clear-headed analysis of the "four" Enlightenments that emerged in colonial and revolutionary America.

Mayer, Henry. *All on Fire: William Lloyd Garrison and the Abolition of Slavery*. New York: St. Martins, 1998. An admiring, almost partisan, but thorough biography of the premier abolitionist.

McCoy, Drew R. *The Last of the Fathers: James Madison and the Republican Legacy*. New York: Cambridge University Press, 1989. Studies the later years and influence of James Madison in the creation of the politics of the early republic.

McCullough, David G. *John Adams*. New York: Simon & Schuster, 2001. A notable and highly sympathetic biography of the second president.

———. *The Presidency of George Washington*. Lawrence, KS: University Press of Kansas, 1974. A careful analysis of the politics of Washington's two administrations.

McDonald, Forrest. *Alexander Hamilton: A Biography*. New York: W.W. Norton, 1979. A detailed and sympathetic treatment of

Hamilton, which is especially illuminating in explaining Hamilton's economic policies as secretary of the treasury.

————. *The Presidency of Thomas Jefferson*. Lawrence, KS: University Press of Kansas, 1976. Part of the University of Kansas *Presidency* series, McDonald surveys Jefferson's two terms in office.

Meyers, Marvin. *The Jacksonian Persuasion: Politics and Belief*. Stanford, CA: Stanford University Press, 1957. Classic study of the political ideas and ideals of Jackson and his followers.

Morgan, Edmund S. *The Puritan Dilemma: The Story of John Winthrop*. Boston: Little, Brown, 1958. One of the great American biographies, it sympathetically portrays Winthrop as a Puritan determined to find a middle ground between moral indifference and moral absolutism in managing public affairs.

Morison, Samuel Eliot. *Builders of the Bay Colony*. Boston: Houghton, Mifflin, 1930. Twelve masterful portraits of the political, religious, economic, and intellectual leaders of the first generation of Massachusetts Bay Puritans, told with the verve of a great narrator.

Morris, Thomas D. *Southern Slavery and the Law, 1619–1860*. Chapel Hill, NC: University of North Carolina Press, 1996. Detailed survey of the legal structures that supported slavery in the slave states of the South.

Murdock, Harold. *Bunker Hill: Notes and Queries on a Famous Battle*. Boston: Houghton Mifflin Company, 1927. A marvelous antiquarian's exploration of the nooks and crannies of a famous revolutionary battle.

Newmyer, R. Kent. *John Marshall and the Heroic Age of the Supreme Court*. Baton Rouge: Louisiana State University Press, 2001. A detailed legal history of the Marshall Court and the cases Marshall used to fashion a central national identity and economic system.

Oakes, James. *The Ruling Race: A History of American Slaveholders*. New York: Random House, 1982. An innovative presentation of competing theories of how slaveowners justified the enslavement and ownership of blacks and the moral stresses that led some to evangelical Protestantism and others to secession.

Onuf, Peter S. *Statehood and Union: A History of the Northwest Ordinance*. Bloomington, IN: Indiana University Press, 1987. A study of how the Confederation Congress dealt with the status and organization of the western territory it won from Great Britain in the Revolution.

Rahe, Paul Anthony. *Republics Ancient and Modern: Classical Republicanism and the American Revolution.* Chapel Hill, NC: University of North Carolina Press, 1992. A staggeringly thorough survey of the political nature and structure of republican governments and their example for the Founding Fathers.

Rakove, Jack N. *The Beginnings of National Politics: An Interpretive History of the Continental Congress.* New York: Knopf, 1979. Portrait of the Continental Congress as a practical, problem-solving body, not so much driven by faction as by the novelty of the dilemmas it faced and the solutions it was politically possible to reach.

Remini, Robert Vincent. *Andrew Jackson and the Course of American Democracy, 1833–1845.* New York: Harper & Row, 1984. The third and final volume of Remini's tremendous survey of the life of Andrew Jackson.

———. *Andrew Jackson and the Course of American Empire* (New York: Harper & Row, 1977).

———. *Andrew Jackson and the Course of American Freedom, 1822–1832* (New York: Harper & Row, 1981).

———. *The Battle of New Orleans.* New York: Viking, 1999. A detailed but face-paced description of the battle that made Andrew Jackson a national hero.

———. *Henry Clay: Statesman for the Union.* New York: W.W. Norton, 1991. The best biography of Clay.

———. *John Quincy Adams.* New York: Times Books, 2002. A brief biography of one of the most gifted, but one of the most politically unfortunate, presidents.

Richardson, Robert D. *Emerson: The Mind on Fire.* Berkeley, CA: University of California Press, 1995. Great biography that links Emerson to the surge of Romanticism in Europe and America.

Rogin, Michael Paul. *Fathers and Children: Andrew Jackson and the Subjugation of the American Indian.* New York: Knopf, 1975. Psychological study of Andrew Jackson that roots his murderous hostility toward Indians in a deep psychic need to see political relationships from the viewpoint of a dominant, patriarchal father.

Schlesinger, Arthur M. *The Age of Jackson*. Boston: Little, Brown, 1945. A classic and admiring survey of Jackson's presidency, casting Jackson in the role of "man of the people" presiding over an early version of the New Deal.

Schoelwer, Susan Prendergast. *Alamo Images: Changing Perceptions of a Texas Experience*. Dallas, TX: Southern Methodist University Press, 1985. History of how our public image of the Alamo as a "shrine" developed in art and architecture.

Schwartz, Seymour I. *The French and Indian War, 1754–1763: The Imperial Struggle for North America*. New York: Simon & Schuster, 1994. Surveys the battles and strategies that gave Great Britain dominance in North America and around the globe.

Sheriff, Carol. *The Artificial River: The Erie Canal and the Paradox of Progress, 1817–1862*. New York: Hill & Wang, 1996. A detailed analytical study of the origins, construction, and functions of the Erie Canal.

Silbey, Joel. *The Partisan Imperative: The Dynamics of American Politics before the Civil War*. New York: Oxford University Press, 1985. Argues for the crucial role played by personal identification with party and the degree to which party loyalty inflamed political contests in the early republic.

Smith, Timothy L. *Revivalism and Social Reform: American Protestantism on the Eve of the Civil War*. Baltimore: Johns Hopkins University Press, 1957, 1980. The classic account of the involvement of evangelical revivalists with social reform movements from 1840 to 1861.

Stampp, Kenneth M. *The Peculiar Institution: Slavery in the Antebellum South*. New York: Knopf, 1956. This book single-handedly rewrote the priorities for understanding slavery and ended a long era in which slavery was looked on as a benign institution.

Steele, Ian K. *Warpaths: Invasions of North America*. New York: Oxford University Press, 1993. A military history of European invasion that argues for the ingenuity and skill of the Indians in rising to meet and defeat European organization and technology.

Taylor, Alan. *American Colonies*. New York: Viking, 2001. Ambitious survey of the entire Americas as colonies, beginning with prehistory and concluding with the Russian and British explorations of Alaska and the Pacific Northwest.

Thomas, Hugh. *The Slave Trade: The Story of the Transatlantic Slave Trade*. New York: Simon & Schuster, 1997. A vast, sprawling narrative, extended over four continents and four centuries, of the traffic in African slaves and its eventual suppression.

Tuveson, Ernest Lee. *Redeemer Nation: The Idea of America's Millennial Role*. Chicago: University of Chicago Press, 1968. A study of America's self-image as divinely ordained to preach a gospel of democracy to the world as a precursor to a golden age of millennial happiness.

Wallace, Anthony F. C. *The Death and Rebirth of the Seneca*. New York: Knopf, 1970. An anthropologist's interpretation of the Handsome Lake religious revival among the Seneca of upstate New York and the suggestion of a paradigm of "revitalization" for understanding the renewal and revival of cultures.

————. *Rockdale: The Growth of an American Village in the Early Industrial Revolution*. New York: Knopf, 1978. Focuses on one mill town in southeastern Pennsylvania to demonstrate the creative and unpredictable mixture of commercial values and evangelical Protestant religion in fostering a community that opposed slavery and eagerly expected the millennium.

Watson, Harry L. *Liberty and Power: The Politics of Jacksonian America*. New York: Hill and Wang, 1990. A short but skillful survey of the shifting tides of political conflict in Jackson's America, with special attention to the underlying cultural values represented by these conflicts.

White, G. Edward. *The Marshall Court and Cultural Change, 1815–1835*. New York: Oxford University Press, 1991. In-depth survey of the legal philosophy and critical decisions of John Marshall and the Supreme Court.

Wilentz, Sean. *Chants Democratic: New York City and the Rise of the American Working Class, 1788–1850*. New York: Oxford University Press, 1984. Chronicles the development of a property-less urban working class and its political organization.

Winslow, Ola Elizabeth. *Jonathan Edwards, 1703–1758: A Biography*. New York: Macmillan, 1940. A Pulitzer Prize winner at its publication and still the finest biography of Edwards available.

Wolf, Stephanie. *As Various as Their Land: The Everyday Lives of Eighteenth-Century Americans*. New York: Harper Collins, 1993. A charming but shrewd survey of the "ordinary" lives of colonial Americans in the home, at work, and in their community.

Wright, Robert. *The Continental Army*. Washington, DC: Center of Military History, 1986. Highly detailed military analysis of the structure and doctrine of Washington's army.

Wright, Ronald. *Stolen Continents: The Americas through Indian Eyes Since 1492*. Boston: Houghton Mifflin, 1992. A powerfully written "alternative" history of the European conquest of the Americas from the point of view of five Indian tribes—the Aztec, Maya, Inca, Cherokee, and Iroquois.

Document Collections:

Allen, W. B., ed. *George Washington: A Collection*. Indianapolis, IN: Liberty Press, 1988. Outstanding single-volume anthology of Washington's writings, mostly letters.

Belz, Herman, ed. *The Webster-Hayne Debate on the Nature of the Union*. Indianapolis, IN: Liberty Fund, 2000. Complete texts of Webster's debates in the Senate with Robert Hayne over the tariff, plus speeches from Thomas Hart Benton, Edward Livingston, and others.

DePauw, Linda G., et al., eds. *Journal of William Maclay*, vol. 9 of the *Documentary History of the First Federal Congress of the United States of America*. Baltimore: Johns Hopkins University Press, 1988. A first-person account of the inner workings of the first Congress under the Constitution.

Dunn, Richard S., and Laetitia Yaendle, eds. *The Journal of John Winthrop, 1630–1649*. Cambridge, MA: Harvard University Press, 1996. The running commentary Winthrop kept from 1629 until close to his death on the founding of the Massachusetts Bay colony; also available in an abridged edition.

Forbes, Allyn B., ed. *The Winthrop Papers*. Boston: Massachusetts Historical Society, 1929–1947, five volumes (1498–1649). Complete compilation of the letters and papers of three generations of Winthrops in England and America.

Freeman, Joanna B., ed. *Alexander Hamilton: Writings*. Library of America, 2001. Best one-volume collection of Hamilton's writings and major state papers as secretary of the treasury.

Howe, Daniel Walker, ed. *The American Whigs: An Anthology*. New York: Wiley, 1973. The only collection of Whig political writings.

Hyneman, Charles S., and Donald Lutz, eds. *American Political Writings during the Founding Era, 1760–1805*. Indianapolis, IN: Liberty Press, 1983, two volumes. A broad collection of American political pamphlets, sermons, and treatises, with the first volume devoted to the revolutionary period and the second, to the Constitution and early republic.

Johnson, Thomas, and Perry Miller, eds. *The Puritans: A Sourcebook of Their Writings*. New York: Harper & Row, 1938, rev. ed., 1963. The most convenient source for a broad sampling of Puritan writing, organized topically in two volumes.

Kline, Mary Jo, ed. *The Political Correspondence and Public Papers of Aaron Burr*. Princeton: Princeton University Press, 1983, two volumes.

Lence, Ross. *Union and Liberty: The Political Philosophy of John C. Calhoun*. Indianapolis, IN: Liberty Fund, 1992. Fourteen of Calhoun's most important writings, including his protests against the "Tariff of Abomination" and the Compromise of 1850.

Oberg, Barbara et al, editors. *The Papers of Thomas Jefferson*. Princeton: Princeton University Press, 1950-, 30 volumes.

Peterson, Merrill D., ed. *The Portable Thomas Jefferson*. New York: Penguin, 1975. The best single-volume collection of Jefferson's papers and letters.

Richardson, James D. ed. *A Compilation of the Messages and Papers of the Presidents, 1789–1897*. Washington, DC: Government Printing Office, 1896–1899. Provides the texts of presidential proclamations, inaugural addresses, annual messages to Congress, and veto messages, from George Washington to William McKinley.

Soderlund, Jean R., ed. *William Penn and the Founding of Pennsylvania, 1680–1684: A Documentary History*. Philadelphia: University of Pennsylvania Press, 1983. Culled from the larger papers of the William Penn project, this single volume collects the most important documents concerning Penn and the creation of the Pennsylvania colony.

Stout, Harry S., gen. ed. *The Works of Jonathan Edwards*. New Haven: Yale University Press, 1957- . A comprehensive edition of Edwards's writings and papers, including sermons, philosophical and theological books, correspondence, and "miscellanies"; currently at 19 volumes.

Syrett, Harold C., et al., eds. *The Papers of Alexander Hamilton*. New York: Columbia University Press, 1961–1981, 27 volumes.

Notes

Notes